THE GEF

MW01174013

IN BELGIUM

An Historical Record

BY

ARNOLD J. TOYNBEE

LATE FELLOW OF BALLIOL COLLEGE,
OXFORD

NEW YORK
GEORGE H. DORAN COMPANY
MCMXVII

PREFACE

THE subject of this book is the treatment of the civil population in the countries overrun by the German Armies during the first three months of the European War. The form of it is a connected narrative, based on the published documents* and reproducing them by direct quotation or (for the sake of brevity) by reference.

With the documents now published on both sides it is at last possible to present a clear narrative of what actually happened. The co-ordination of this mass of evidence, which has gradually accumulated since the first days of invasion, is the principal purpose for which the book has been written. The evidence consists of first-hand statements—some delivered on oath before a court, others taken down from the witnesses without oath by competent legal examiners, others written and published on the witnesses' own initiative as books or pamphlets. Most of them originally appeared in print in a controversial setting, as proofs or disproofs of disputed fact, or as justifications or condemnations of fact that was admitted. In the present work, however, this argumentative aspect of them has been avoided as far as possible. For it has either been treated exhaustively in official publications

* A schedule of the more important documents will be found in the "List of Abbreviations" pp. xi-xiii.

—the case of Louvain, for instance, in the German White Book and the Belgian Reply to it—or will not be capable of such treatment till after the conclusion of the War. The ultimate inquiry and verdict, if it is to have finality, must proceed either from a mixed commission of representatives of all the States concerned, or from a neutral commission like that appointed by the Carnegie Foundation to inquire into the atrocities committed during the Balkan War. But the German Government has repeatedly refused proposals, made both unofficially and officially, that it should allow such an investigation to be conducted in the territory at present under German military occupation,* and the final critical assessment will therefore necessarily be postponed till the German Armies have retired again within their own frontiers.

Meanwhile, an ordered and documented narrative of the attested facts seems the best preparation for that judicial appraisement for which the time is not yet ripe. The facts have been drawn from statements made by witnesses on opposite sides with different intentions and beliefs, but as far as possible they have been disengaged from this subjective setting and have been set out, without comment, to speak for themselves. It has been impossible, however, to confine the exposition to pure narration at every point, for in the original evidence the facts observed and the inferred explanation of them are seldom distinguished, and when the same observed fact is made a ground for diametrically opposite inferences by different witnesses, the difficulty becomes acute. A German soldier, say, in Louvain on

---

* Belgian Reply pp. vii. and 97-8.

the night of August 25th, 1914, hears the sound of machine-gun firing apparently coming from a certain spot in the town, and infers that at this spot Belgian civilians are using a machine gun against German troops; a Belgian inhabitant hears the same sound, and infers that German troops are firing on civilians. In such cases the narrative must be interpreted by a judgment as to which of the inferences is the truth, and this judgment involves discussion. What is remarkable, however, is the rarity of these contradictions. Usually the different testimonies fit together into a presentation of fact which is not open to argument.

The narrative has been arranged so as to follow separately the tracks of the different German Armies or groups of Armies which traversed different sectors of French and Belgian territory. Within each sector the chronological order has been followed, which is generally identical with the geographical order in which the places affected lie along the route of march. The present volume describes the invasion of Belgium up to the sack of Louvain.

ARNOLD J. TOYNBEE.

March, 1917.

CONTENTS

FRONTISPIECE . . . . *The Invaded Country (Map)*

PAGE

PREFACE v

TABLE OF CONTENTS. ix

LIST OF MAPS ix

LIST OF ILLUSTRATIONS x

LIST OF ABBREVIATIONS xi

CHAPTER I.: THE TRACK OF THE ARMIES 15

CHAPTER II.: FROM THE FRONTIER TO LIÉGE . . 23

    (i) ON THE VISÉ ROAD 23
    (ii) ON THE BARCHON ROAD 27
    (iii) ON THE FLÉRON ROAD 31
    (iv) ON THE VERVIERS ROAD 37
    (v) ON THE MALMÉDY ROAD 38
    (vi) BETWEEN THE VESDRE AND THE OURTHE 42
    (vii) ACROSS THE MEUSE 44
    (viii) THE CITY OF LIÉGE 46

CHAPTER III.: FROM LIÉGE TO MALINES 52

    (i) THROUGH LIMBURG TO AERSCHOT 52
    (ii) AERSCHOT 57
    (iii) THE AERSCHOT DISTRICT 74
    (iv) THE RETREAT FROM MALINES 77
    (v) LOUVAIN 89

MAPS

THE INVADED COUNTRY . . . . *Frontispiece*

THE TRACK OF THE ARMIES: FROM THE
    FRONTIER TO MALINES* . . . . . . *End of Volume*

LOUVAIN, FROM THE GERMAN WHITE BOOK *End of Volume*

* *This map shows practically all the roads and places referred to in the text.*

ILLUSTRATIONS

		PAGE
1.	MOULAND . . . . *To face page*	16
2.	BATTICE	17
3.	LIÉGE FORTS: A DESTROYED CUPOLA	32
4.	ANS: AN INTERIOR	33
5.	ANS: THE CHURCH	48
6.	LIÉGE: A FARM HOUSE	49
7.	LIÉGE UNDER GERMAN OCCUPATION . . . , . . .	52
8.	LIÉGE UNDER THE GERMANS: RUINS AND PLACARDS . .	53
9.	LIÉGE IN RUINS	60
10.	"WE LIVE LIKE GOD IN BELGIUM"	61
11.	HAELEN	64
12.	AERSCHOT	65
13.	BRUSSELS: A BOOKING-OFFICE	80
14.	MALINES AFTER BOMBARDMENT	81
15.	MALINES: RUINS	84
16.	MALINES: RUINS	85
17.	MALINES: CARDINAL MERCIER'S STATE-ROOM AS A RED CROSS HOSPITAL	92
18.	MALINES: THE CARDINAL'S THRONE-ROOM	93
19.	CAPELLE-AU-BOIS	96
20.	CAPELLE-AU-BOIS	97
21.	CAPELLE-AU-BOIS: THE CHURCH	112
22.	LOUVAIN: NEAR THE CHURCH OF ST. PIERRE	113
23.	LOUVAIN: THE CHURCH OF ST. PIERRE	116
24.	LOUVAIN: THE CHURCH OF ST. PIERRE ACROSS THE RUINS	117
25.	LOUVAIN: THE CHURCH OF ST. PIERRE—INTERIOR . . .	124
26.	LOUVAIN: STATION SQUARE	125

ABBREVIATIONS

ALPHABET, LETTERS OF THE:—

CAPITALS . . Appendices to the German White Book entitled: "*The Violation of International Law in the Conduct of the Belgian People's-War*" (dated Berlin, 10th May, 1915): Arabic numerals after the capital letter refer to the depositions contained in each Appendix.

LOWER CASE . Sections of the "*Appendix to the Report of the Committee on Alleged German Outrages, Appointed by His Britannic Majesty's Government and Presided Over by the Right Hon. Viscount Bryce, O.M.*" (Cd. 7895); Arabic numerals after the lower case letter refer to the depositions contained in each Section.

ANN(EX) . . . Annexes (numbered 1 to 9) to the *Reports of the Belgian Commission* (*vide infra*).

BELG. . . . . *Reports (numbered i to xxii) of the Official Commission of the Belgian Government on the Violation of the Rights of Nations and of the Laws and Customs of War.* (English translation, published, on behalf of the Belgian Legation, by H.M. Stationery Office, two volumes.)

BLAND . . . . "*Germany's Violations of the Laws of War, 1914–5*"; compiled under the Auspices of the French Ministry of Foreign Affairs, and translated into English with an Introduction by J. O. P. Bland. (London: Heinemann. 1915.)

BRYCE . . . . *Appendix to the Report of the Committee on Alleged German Outrages appointed by His Britannic Majesty's Government.*

CHAMBRY . . . "*The Truth about Louvain*," by Réné Chambry. (Hodder and Stoughton. 1915.)

xi

ABBREVIATIONS

DAVIGNON . . . "*Belgium and Germany*," Texts and Documents, preceded by a Foreword by Henri Davignon. (Thomas Nelson and Sons.)

"EYE-WITNESS" . "*An Eye-Witness at Louvain.*" (London: Eyre and Spottiswoode. 1914.)

"GERMANS" . . "*The Germans at Louvain*," by a volunteer worker in the *Hôpital St.-Thomas.* (Hodder and Stoughton. 1916.)

GRONDIJS . . . "*The Germans in Belgium: Experiences of a Neutral*," by L. H. Grondijs, Ph.D., formerly Professor of Physics at the Technical Institute of Dordrecht. (London: Heinemann. 1915.)

HÖCKER . . . . "*An der Spitze Meiner Kompagnie, Three Months of Campaigning*," by Paul Oskar Höcker. (Ullstein and Co., Berlin and Vienna. 1914.)

"HORRORS" . . . "*The Horrors of Louvain*," by an Eye-witness, with an Introduction by Lord Halifax. (Published by the London *Sunday Times.*)

MASSART . . . "*Belgians under the German Eagle*," by Jean Massart, Vice-Director of the Class of Sciences in the Royal Academy of Belgium. (English translation by Bernard Miall. London: Fisher Unwin. 1916.)

MERCIER . . . *Pastoral Letter*, dated Xmas, 1914, of His Eminence Cardinal Mercier, Archbishop of Malines.

MORGAN . . . . "*German Atrocities: An Official Investigation*," by J. H. Morgan, M.A., Professor of Constitutional Law in the University of London. (London: Fisher Unwin. 1916.)

NUMERALS, ROMAN LOWER CASE . . *Reports (numbered i to xxii) of the Belgian Commission (vide supra).*

R(EPLY) . . . . "*Reply to the German White Book of May 10, 1915.*" (Published, for the Belgian Ministry of Justice and Ministry of Foreign Affairs, by Berger-Levrault, Paris, 1916.)
Arabic numerals after the *R* refer to the depositions contained in the particular section of the *Reply* that is being cited at the moment: *e.g.*, R15 denotes the fifteenth deposition in the sec-

tion on Louvain in the *Reply* when cited in the section on Louvain in the present work; but it denotes the fifteenth deposition in the section on Aerschot when cited in the corresponding section here.

The *Reply* is also referred to by pages, and in these cases the Arabic numeral denotes the page and is preceded by "p."

S(OMVILLE) . . . *"The Road to Liége,"* by Gustave Somville. (English translation by Bernard Miall. Hodder and Stoughton. 1916.)

STRUYKEN . . . *"The German White Book on the War in Belgium: A Commentary,"* by Professor A. A. H. Struyken. (English Translation of Articles in the Journal *Van Onzen Tijd*, of Amsterdam, July 31st, August 7th, 14th, 21st, 1915. Thomas Nelson and Sons.)

N.B.—Statistics, where no reference is given, are taken from the first and second Annexes to the Reports of the Belgian Commission. They are based on official investigations.

THE GERMAN TERROR
IN BELGIUM

I. THE TRACK OF THE ARMIES.

WHEN Germany declared war upon Russia, Belgium, and France in the first days of August, 1914, German armies immediately invaded Russian, Belgian, and French territory, and as soon as the frontiers were crossed, these armies began to wage war, not merely against the troops and fortifications of the invaded states, but against the lives and property of the civil population.

Outrages of this kind were committed during the whole advance and retreat of the Germans through Belgium and France, and only abated when open manœuvring gave place to trench warfare along all the line from Switzerland to the sea. Similar outrages accompanied the simultaneous advance into the western salient of Russian Poland, and the autumn incursion of the Austro-Hungarians into Serbia, which was turned back at Valievo. There was a remarkable uniformity in the crimes committed in these widely separated theatres of war, and an equally remarkable limit to the dates within which they fell. They all occurred during the first three months of the war, while, since that period, though outrages have continued, they have not been of the same character or on the same scale. This has not been due to the immobility of the fronts, for although it is certainly true that the Germans have been unable to overrun fresh territories on the west, they have carried out greater invasions than ever in Russia and the Balkans, which have not been marked by outrages of the same specific kind. This seems to show that the systematic warfare against the civil population in the campaigns of 1914 was the result of policy, deliberately tried and afterwards deliberately given up. The hypothesis would account for the peculiar features in the German Army's conduct, but before we can understand these features we must survey the sum of what the Germans did. The catalogue of crimes against civilians extends through every phase and theatre of the military operations in the first three months of the war, and an outline of these is a necessary introduction to it.

In August, 1914, the Central Empires threw their main strength against Belgium and France, and penetrated far further on this front than on the east and south-east. The line on which they advanced extended from the northern end of the Vosges to the Dutch frontier on the Meuse, and here again their strength was unevenly distributed. The chief striking force was

L. MOULAND

2. BATTICE

concentrated in the extreme north, and advanced in an immense arc across the Meuse, the Scheldt, the Somme, and the Oise to the outskirts of Paris. As this right wing pressed forward, one army after another took up the movement toward the left or south-eastern flank, but each made less progress than its right-hand neighbour. While the first three armies from the right all crossed the Marne before they were compelled to retreat, the fourth (the Crown Prince's) never reached it, and the army of Lorraine was stopped a few miles within French territory, before ever it crossed the Meuse. We shall set down very briefly the broad movements of these armies and the dates on which they took place.

Germany sent her ultimatum to Belgium on the evening of Aug. 2nd. It announced that Germany would violate Belgian neutrality within twelve hours, unless Belgium betrayed it herself, and it was rejected by Belgium the following morning. That day Germany declared war on France, and the next day, Aug. 4th, the advance guard of the German right wing crossed the Belgian frontier and attacked the *forts of Liége*. On Aug. 7th the town of *Liége* was entered, and the crossings of the Meuse, from Liége to the Dutch frontier, were in German hands.

Beyond Liége the invading forces spread out like a fan. On the extreme right a force advanced north-west to outflank the Belgian army covering Brussels and to mask the fortress of Antwerp, and this right wing, again, was the first to move. Its van was defeated by the Belgians at *Haelen* on Aug. 12th, but the main column entered *Hasselt* on the same day, and took *Aerschot* and *Louvain* on Aug. 19th. During the next few days it pushed on to *Malines*, was driven out again by a Belgian sortie from Antwerp on Aug. 25th, but retook Malines before the end of the month, and contained the Antwerp garrison along the line of the Dyle and the Démer.

This was all that the German right flank column was intended to do, for it was only a subsidiary part of the two armies concentrated at Liége. As soon as Antwerp was covered, the mass of these armies was launched westward from Liége into the gap between the fortresses of Antwerp and Namur—von Kluck's army on the right and von Bülow's on the left. By Aug. 21st von Bülow was west of Namur, and attacking the French on the *Sambre*. On Aug. 20th an army corps of von Kluck's had paraded through *Brussels*, and on the 23rd his main body, wheeling southwest, attacked the British at *Mons*. On the 24th von Kluck's extreme right reached the Scheldt at *Tournai* and, under this threat to their left flank, the British and French abandoned their positions on the Mons-Charleroi line and retreated to the south. Von Kluck and von Bülow hastened in pursuit. They passed *Cambrai* on Aug. 26th and *St. Quentin* on the 29th; on the

31st von Kluck was crossing the Oise at *Compiègne*, and on the 6th Sept. he reached his furthest point at *Courchamp*, south-east of Paris and nearly thirty miles beyond the *Marne*. His repulse, like his advance, was brought about by an outflanking manœuvre, only this time the Anglo-French had the initiative, and it was von Kluck who was outflanked. His retirement compelled von Bülow to fall back on his left, after a bloody defeat in the marshes of *St. Gond*, and the retreat was taken up, successively, by the other armies which had come into line on the left of von Bülow.

These armies had all crossed the Meuse south of the fortress of Namur, and, to retain connexion with them, von Bülow had had to detach a force on his left to seize the line of the Meuse from Liége to Namur and to capture Namur itself. The best German heavy artillery was assigned to this force for the purpose, and *Namur* fell, after an unexpectedly short bombardment, on Aug. 23rd, while Von Bülow's main army at Charleroi was still engaged in its struggle with the French.

The fall of Namur opened the way for German armies to cross the Meuse along the whole line from Namur to Verdun. The first crossing was made at *Dinant* on Aug. 23rd, the very day on which Namur fell, by a Saxon army, which marched thither by cross routes through Luxembourg; the second by the Duke of Würtemberg's army between *Mezières* and *Sedan;* and the third by the Crown Prince of Prussia's army immediately north of *Verdun*. West of the Meuse the Saxons and Würtembergers amalgamated, and got into touch with von Bülow on their right. Advancing parallel with him, they reached *Charleville* on Aug. 25th, crossed the Aisne at *Rethel* on the 30th and the Marne at *Châlons* on the 4th, and were stopped on the 7th at *Vitry en Perthois*. The Crown Prince, on their left, did not penetrate so far. Instead of the plains of Champagne he had to traverse the hill country of the *Argonne*. He turned back at *Sermaize*, which he had reached on Sept. 6th, and never saw the Marne.

On the left of the Crown Prince a Bavarian army crossed the frontier between Metz and the Vosges. Its task was to join hands with the Crown Prince round the southern flank of Verdun, as the Duke of Würtemberg had joined hands with von Bülow round the flank of Namur. But Verdun never fell, and the Bavarian advance was the weakest of any. *Lunéville* fell on Aug. 22nd, and *Baccarat* was entered on the 24th; but *Nancy* was never reached, and on Sept. 12th the general German retreat extended to this south-easternmost sector, and the Bavarians fell back.

Thus the German invading armies were everywhere checked and driven back between the 6th and the 12th September, 1914. The operations which came to this issue bear the general name of the *Battle of the Marne*. The *Marne* was followed immediately by the *Aisne*, and the issue of the Aisne was a change from open to trench warfare along a line extending from the Vosges to the Oise. This change was complete before September closed, and the line formed then has remained practically unaltered to the present time. But there was another month of open fighting between the Oise and the sea.

When the Germans' strategy was defeated at the Marne, they transferred their efforts to the north-west, and took the initiative there. On Sept. 9th the Belgian Army had made a second sortie from Antwerp, to coincide with the counter-offensive of Joffre, and this time they had even reoccupied *Aerschot*. The Germans retaliated by taking the offensive on the Scheldt. The retaining army before Antwerp was strongly reinforced. Its left flank was secured, in the latter half of September, by the occupation of *Termonde* and *Alost*. The attack on *Antwerp* itself began on Sept. 27th. On the 2nd the outer ring of forts was forced, and on the 9th the Germans entered the city. The towns of Flanders fell in rapid succession—*Ghent* on the 12th, *Bruges* on the 14th, *Ostend* on the 15th—and the Germans hoped to break through to the Channel ports on the front between Ostend and the Oise. Meanwhile, each side had been feverishly extending its lines from the Oise towards the north and pushing forward cavalry to turn the exposed flank of the opponent. These two simultaneous movements—the extension of the trench lines from the Oise to the sea, and the German thrust across

Flanders to the Channel—intersected one another at *Ypres*, and the *Battle of Ypres and the Yser*, in the latter part of October, was the crisis of this north-western struggle. On Oct. 31st the German effort to break through reached, and passed, its climax, and trench warfare established itself as decisively from the Oise to the sea as it had done a month earlier between the Vosges and the Oise.

Thus, three months after the German armies crossed the frontier, the German invasion of Belgium and France gave place to a permanent German occupation of French and Belgian territories behind a practically stationary front, and with this change of character in the fighting a change came over the outrages upon the civil population which remained in Germany's power. The crimes of the invasion and the crimes of the occupation are of a different order from one another, and must be dealt with apart.

II. FROM THE FRONTIER TO LIÉGE.

(i) *On the Visé Road.*

The Germans invaded Belgium on Aug. 4th, 1914. Their immediate objective was the fortress of Liége and the passage of the Meuse, but first they had to cross a zone of Belgian territory from twenty to twenty-five miles wide. They came over the frontier along four principal roads, which led through this territory to the fortress and the river, and this is what they did in the towns and villages they passed.

The first road led from Aix-la-Chapelle, in Germany, to the bridge over the Meuse at Visé, skirting the Dutch frontier, and *Warsage** was the first Belgian village on this road to which the Germans came. Their advance-guards distributed a proclamation by General von Emmich: *"I give formal pledges to the Belgian popu-lation that they will not have to suffer from the hor-rors of war. . . . If you wish to avoid the horrors of war, you must act wisely and with a true appreciation of your duty to your country."* This was on the morn-ing of Aug. 4th, and the Mayor of Warsage, M. Fléchet, had already posted a notice on the town-hall

*Belgian Report xvi (statements by the Mayor and another inhab-itant) ; Somville pp. 134-143.

warning the inhabitants to keep calm. All that day
and the next the Germans passed through; on the afternoon of the 6th the village was clear of them, when
suddenly they swarmed back, shooting in at the windows and setting houses on fire. Several people were
killed; one old man was burnt alive. Then the Mayor
was ordered to assemble the population in the square.
A German officer had been shot on the road. No inquiry was held; no post-mortem examination made (the
German soldiers were nervous and marched with finger
on trigger); the village was condemned. The houses
were systematically plundered, and then systematically
burnt. A dozen inhabitants, including the Burgomaster, were carried off as hostages to the German camp
at Mouland. Three were shot at once; the rest were
kept all night in the open; one of them was tied to a
cart-wheel and beaten with rifle-butts; in the morning
six were hanged, the rest set free. Eighteen people
in all were killed at Warsage and 25 houses destroyed.

At *Fouron-St. Martin** five people were killed and
20 houses burnt. Nineteen houses were burnt at
Fouron-le-Compte.* At *Berneau,*† a few miles further
down the road, 67 houses (out of 116) were burnt on
Aug. 5th, and 7 people killed. "The people of Berneau," writes a German in his diary on Aug. 5th, "have

* Belg. xvii.
† Somville pp. 143-6.

fired on those who went to get water. The village has
been partly destroyed." On the day of this entry the
Germans had commandeered wine at Berneau, and were
drunk when they took reprisals for shots their victims ·
were never proved to have fired. Among these victims
was the Burgomaster, M. Bruyère, a man of 83. He
was taken, like the Burgomaster of Warsage, to the
camp at Mouland, and was never seen again after the
night of the 6th. At *Mouland* * itself 4 people were
killed and 73 houses destroyed (out of 132).

The road from Aix-la-Chapelle reaches the Meuse
at *Visé.*† It was a town of 900 houses and 4,000 souls,
and, as a German describes it, "It vanished from the
map." ‡ The inhabitants were killed, scattered or deported, the houses levelled to the ground, and this was
done systematically, stage by stage.

The Germans who marched through Warsage
reached Visé on the afternoon of Aug. 4th. The Belgians had blown up the bridges at Visé and Argenteau,
and were waiting for the Germans on the opposite bank.
As they entered Visé, the Germans came for the first
time under fire, and they wreaked their vengeance on
the town. "The first house they came to as they entered
Visé they burned" (a 16), and they began to fire at
random in the streets. At least eight civilians were

* Somville pp. 146-7.
† Belg. xvii; Somville pp. 177-184; Bland pp. 164-5; a 16.
‡ Höcker p. 46.

shot in this way before night, and when night fell the population was driven out of the houses and compelled to bivouac in the square. More houses were burnt on the 6th; on the 10th they burned the church; on the 11th they seized the Dean, the Burgomaster, and the Mother Superior of the Convent as hostages; on the 15th a regiment of East Prussians arrived and was billeted in the town, and that night Visé was destroyed. "I saw commissioned officers directing and supervising the burning," says an inhabitant (a 16). "It was done systematically with the use of benzine, spread on the floors and then lighted. In my own and another house I saw officers come in before the burning with revolvers in their hands, and have china, valuable antique furniture, and other such things removed. This being done, the houses were, by their orders, set on fire. . . ."

The East Prussians were drunk, there was firing in the streets, and, once more, people were killed. Next morning the population was rounded up in the station square and sorted out—men this side, women that. The women might go to Holland, the men, in two gangs of about 300 each, were deported to Germany as franc-tireurs. "During the night of Aug. 15-16," as another German diarist* describes the scene, "Pioneer Grimbow gave the alarm in the town of Visé. Everyone was shot or taken prisoner, and the houses were burnt. The prisoners were made to march and keep up with

---

* Bland p. 165.

the troops." About 30 people in all were killed at Visé, and 575 out of 876 houses destroyed. On the final day of destruction the Germans had been in peaceable occupation of the place for ten days, and the Belgian troops had retired about forty miles out of range.

That is what the Germans did on the road from Aix-la-Chapelle; but, before reaching Warsage, the road sends out a branch through Aubel to the left, which passes under the guns of *Fort Barchon* and leads straight to Liége. The Germans took this road also, and Barchon was the first of the Liége forts to fall. The civil population was not spared.

(ii) *On the Barchon Road.*

At *St. André,** 4 civilians were killed and 14 houses burnt. *Julémont,†* the next village, was completely plundered and burnt. Only 2 houses remained standing, and 12 people were killed. Advancing along this road, the Germans arrived at *Blégny‡* on Aug. 5th. Several inhabitants of Blégny were murdered that afternoon, among them M. Smets, a professor of gunsmithry (the villagers worked for the small-arms manufacturers of Liége). M. Smets was killed in his house, where his wife was in child-bed. The corpse was thrown into the street, the mother and new-born

---

* Somville p. 148.
† Somville pp. 147-8.
‡ Somville pp. 157-168; a 7, 20.

baby were dragged out after it. That night the population of Blégny was herded together in the village institute; their houses were set on fire. Next morning—the 6th—the women were released and the men driven forward by the German infantry towards Barchon fort. The Curé of Blégny, the Abbé Labeye, was among the number, and there were 296 of them in all. In front of Barchon they were placed in rows of four, but the fort would not fire upon this living screen, and they were marched away across country towards Battice, where five were shot before the eyes of the rest, and the curé kicked, spat upon, and pricked with bayonets. They were again driven forward as a screen against a Belgian patrol, and were kept in the open all night. Next morning 4 more were shot—two who had been wounded by the Belgian fire, and one who had heart disease and was too feeble to go on. The fourth was an old man of 78. The Germans tortured these victims by placing lighted cigarettes in their nostrils and ears. After this second execution on the 7th, the remainder were set free. . . .

On the 10th Aug. the curé writes in his diary:

"There are now 38 houses burnt, and 23 damaged.

"Thursday the 13th: a few houses pillaged, two young men taken away.

"Friday, the 14th: a few houses pillaged.

"Friday night: the village of Barchon is burnt and the curé taken prisoner . . . . . . "

The curé's last notes for a sermon have survived: "My brothers, perhaps we shall again see happy days . . ." But on the 16th, before the sermon was delivered, the curé was shot. He was shot against the church wall, with M. Ruwet, the Burgomaster, and two brothers, one of them a revolver manufacturer who had handed over his stock to the German authorities (from whom he received two passes) and had been working for the Red Cross. After the execution the church was burnt down. The nuns of Blégny were shot at by Germans in a motor-car when they came out that day to bury the bodies. From the 5th to the 16th Aug., about 30 people were killed in the commune of Blégny-Trembleur, and 45 houses burnt in all.

The village of *Barchon*,* as the curé of Blégny records, was destroyed on the 14th—in cold blood, five days after the surrender of the fort. There was a battue by two German regiments through the village. The houses were plundered and burnt (110 burnt in all out of 146); the inhabitants were rounded up. Twenty-two were shot in one batch, including two little girls of two and an old woman of ninety-four. Thirty-two perished altogether, and a dozen hostages were carried off, some of whom were tied to field guns and compelled to keep up with the horses. On the 16th the Germans evicted the inhabitants of *Chefneux*,† and

---

* Somville pp. 152-7; xvii.
† Somville p. 156.

... . On the 17th they burned all the 22 houses
... ... At *Saives** they burned 12 houses, and
.... . man and a girl.

We have the diary of a German soldier who marched
over this branch road from Aubel when all the villages had been destroyed except *Wandre*,† which stood
where the road debouched upon the Meuse.

"... Aug.—11:50 a.m. Crossed the Belgian fron-
ter and kept steadily along the high road until we got
into Belgium. We were hardly into it before we met
. terrible sight. Houses were burnt down, the inhabitants driven out and some of them shot. Of the
hundreds of houses not a single one had been spared—
every one was plundered and burnt down. Hardly
were we through this big village when the next was
already set on fire, and so it went on. . . .

"16th Aug. The big village of Barchon set on fire.
The same day, about 11.50 a.m., we came to the town
of Wandre. Here the houses were spared but all
searched. At last we had got out of the town when
once more everything was sent to ruins. In one house
a whole arsenal had been discovered. The inhabitants
were one and all dragged out and shot, but this shooting was absolutely heart-rending, for they all knelt
and prayed. But this got them no mercy. A few shots

* S. p. 148; xvii.
† Bryce pp. 161-2; S. pp. 168-177.

rang out, and they fell backwards into the green grass and went to their eternal sleep.

"And still the brigands would not leave off shooting us from behind—that, and never from in front—but now we could stand it no longer, and raging and roaring we went on and on, and everything that got in our way was smashed or burnt or shot. At last we had to go into bivouac. Half tired out and done up we laid ourselves down, and we didn't wait long before quenching some of our thirst. But we only drank wine; the water has been half poisoned and half left alone by the beasts. Well, we have much too much here to eat and drink. When a pig shows itself anywhere or a hen or a duck or pigeons, they are all shot down and slaughtered, so that at any rate we have something to eat. It is a real adventure. . . ."

This was the temper of the Germans who destroyed Wandre. They burned 33 houses altogether and shot 32 people—16 of them in one batch.

(iii) *On the Fléron Road.*

There is another road from Aix-la-Chapelle to Liége, which passes through Battice and is commanded by *Fort Fléron* (Fort Fléron offered the most determined resistance of all the forts of Liége, and cost the Germans the greatest loss). The Germans marched through *Battice* on August 4th, and came under fire of the fort that afternoon. In the evening they arrested

31

three men in the streets of Battice, and shot them without charge or investigation.

The check to their arms was avenged on the civil population. "On the arrival of the German troops in the village of *Micheroux*," states a Belgian witness (a 12), "during the time when Fort Fléron was holding out, they came to a block of four cottages, and having turned out the inhabitants, set the cottages on fire and burned them. From one of the cottages a woman (mentioned by name) came out with a baby in her arms, and a German soldier snatched it from her and dashed it to the ground, killing it then and there."*

"The position was dangerous," writes a German in his diary† on August 5th, from a picket in front of Fort Fléron. "As suspicious civilians were hovering round, houses 1, 2, 3, 4, 5 were cleared, the owners arrested (and shot the next day). . . . I shoot a civilian with my rifle, at 400 metres, slap through the head. . . ."

That day the curé of Battice‡ (who had been kept under arrest in the open since the evening of the 4th) was driven, with the Mayor and one of the communal councillors, under the Belgian fire. On the 6th the German troops again retired on Battice in confusion, and the village was destroyed that afternoon. Shots were

---

* Same incident recorded in xvii, p. 50.

† Bryce pp. 168-9.

‡ S. pp. 46-55; xvii; Reply pp. 110-116 (Report of L'Abbé Voisin, Curé of Battice, to the Belgian Government).

3. LIÉGE FORTS: A DESTROYED CUPOLA

4. ANS: AN INTERIOR

fired indiscriminately and the houses set on fire. The first victim was a young man sitting in a café with his *fiancée*—he fell dead by her side. Three people were taken to the field to which the men of Blégny had been brought, and were shot with the five victims there. On the 7th they shot a workman who had been given a safe-conduct by a German officer to buy bread in a neighbouring village, and was on his way home with his wife. On the 8th they set the fire going again, to burn what still remained. They burned 146 houses and killed 36 people in Battice from first to last.

The town of *Herve** lies a mile or so beyond Battice on the Fléron road, and was also traversed by the Germans on August 4th. The first to pass were officers in a motor car, and as they crossed the bridge they shot down two young men standing by the roadside— one was badly wounded, the other killed outright. In the evening they sent for the Mayor, accused the inhabitants of having fired on German troops, and threatened to shoot the inhabitants and burn the town to the ground. The Mayor and the curé spent the night going from house to house and warning the people to avoid all grounds of offence—before they had finished there were more shots fired indiscriminately (by the Germans), and more (civilian) wounded and dead. The Mayor and curé were then retained as hostages for the civilians' good behaviour. On the 6th

* S. pp. 55-72; xvii; Reply pp. 123-7; a 2.

the first house was burnt; on the 7th five men were shot in cold blood; on the 8th a fresh column of troops arrived from Aix-la-Chapelle, and these were the destroyers of Herve. "They fired indiscriminately in all quarters of the town," says an eye-witness (a 2), "and in the Rue de la Station they shot Madame Hendrickx, hitting her at close range, although she had a crucifix in her hand—begging for mercy." All through the 8th the shooting and burning went on, and on the 9th the fires were kindled again. "The Germans gave themselves up to pillage and loaded motor cars with everything of value they could find." They burned and pillaged consecutively for ten days, and on the 19th and 20th fresh regiments arrived and carried on the work. Two hundred and seventy-nine houses were destroyed at Herve altogether, and 44 people killed. "On the road to Herve everything is burnt," writes a German soldier (Reply p. 127) who passed when all was over. "At Herve, the same. Everything is burnt except a convent—everywhere corpses carbonised into an indistinguishable mass. (There are about a hundred, all civilians, and children among the number.) I only saw three people alive in the village—an old man, a sister of charity, and a girl." The Belgian witness quoted above (a 2) records that "the German staff officers staying in his hotel told his wife that the reason why they had so treated Herve was because the

34

inhabitants of the town would not petition for a passage for the Germans at Fléron."

In the villages between Herve and Fort Fléron the slaughter and devastation were, if possible, more complete. At *la Bouxhe-Melen** there were two massacres —one on Aug. 5th and another on the 8th. In the second the people were shot down in a field *en masse*, and 129 were murdered altogether, as well as about 40 people herded in from the farms and hamlets of the neighbourhood. Sixty houses in la Bouxhe-Melen were destroyed. In the commune of *Soumagne*,† on a branch road to the south, the Germans killed 165 civilians and burned 104 houses down. When they entered Soumagne on Aug. 5th, they killed indiscriminately in the streets. "They broke the windows and broke the door," writes a witness (a 5) who had taken refuge in a cellar. "My mother went out of the cellar door. . . . Then I heard a shot and my mother fell back into the cellar. She was killed." This indiscriminate killing was followed up the same afternoon by the massacre of 69 civilians in a field called the Fonds Leroy. "The soldiers fired a volley and killed many, and then fired twice more. Then they went through the ranks and bayonetted everyone still living. I saw many bayonetted in this way" (a 4). One boy was shot and bayonetted in four places, and lay

* S. pp. 73-9; xvii.
† S. pp. 113-126; xvii; a 4, 5, 9.

several days among the dead, keeping himself alive on weeds and grass. This boy survived. In another field 18 were massacred in one batch, in another 19. "I saw about 20 dead bodies lying here and there along the road," writes one of the witnesses (a 4). "One of them was that of a little girl aged 13. The rest were men, and most of them had had their heads bashed in." —"I saw 56 corpses of civilians in a meadow," deposes another. "Some had been killed by bayonet thrusts and others by rifle shots. In the heaps of corpses above mentioned was that of the son of the Burgomaster. His throat had been cut from ear to ear and his tongue had been pulled out and cut off."

In the hamlet of *Fécher* the whole population— about 1,000 women, children and men—was penned into the church on Aug. 5th, and next morning the men (412 of them) were herded off as a living screen for the German troops advancing between the forts (the first man to come out of the church being wantonly shot down as an example to the rest). The 411 were driven by bye-roads to the Chartreuse Monastery, above the Meuse, overlooking the bridge into the city of Liége, and on the 7th they were planted as hostages on the bridge while the Germans marched across. They were held there without food or shelter or relief for a hundred hours. At *Micheroux** 9 people were killed and 17 houses destroyed. These villages were all out-

---

* S. pp. 110-2; xvii; a 12.

side the eastern line of forts, but the places inside the line, between the forts and Liége, were devastated to an equal degree. At *Fléron** 15 civilians were killed and 152 houses destroyed.† At *Retinnes*‡ 41 civilians were killed and 118 houses destroyed.† At *Queue du Bois*§ 11 civilians were killed and 35 houses destroyed. At *Evegnée* 2 civilians were killed and 5 houses destroyed. At *Cerexhe*‖ 4 women and children were burnt alive in a house, and 2 houses destroyed. At *Bellaire*¶ 4 people were killed and 15 houses destroyed. At *Jupille*** 8 people were killed and 1 house destroyed. These villages were saved none of the horrors of war by the surrender of the forts.

(iv) *On the Verviers Road.*

The Germans converged on the forts by more southerly roads as well. At *Dolhain*,†† on the road from Eupen to Verviers, 28 houses were burnt on Aug. 8th and several civilians killed. At *Metten*,‡‡ near Verviers, a German soldier confesses that he and his comrades "were ordered to search a house from which shots had

---

* S. pp. 126-130.
† Partly by bombardment during the attack on the fort.
‡ S. pp. 105-110; Reply pp. 133-4.
§ S. pp. 151-2.
‖ S. p. 148.
¶ S. p. 152.
** S. p. 149.
†† xvii. p. 57.
‡‡ Bland pp. 105-9.

been fired, but found nothing in the house but two women and a child. . . . I did not see the women fire. The women were told that nothing would be done to them, because they were crying so bitterly. We brought the women out and took them to the major, and then we were ordered to shoot the women. . . . When the mother was dead, the major gave the order to shoot the child, so that the child should not be left alone in the world. The child's eyes were bandaged. I took part in this because we were ordered to do it by Major Kastendick and Captain Dultingen. . . ."

But Verviers and the Verviers road remained comparatively unscathed. Far worse was done by the Germans who descended on the Vesdre from Malmédy, south-eastward, over the hills.

(v) *On the Malmédy Road.*

*Francorchamps,** the first Belgian village on the Malmédy road, was sacked on Aug. 8th, four days after the first German troops had passed through it unopposed, and again on Aug. 14th by later detachments. At *Hockay,†* near Francorchamps, the curé was shot. In Hockay and Francorchamps 13 people were killed altogether, and 25 houses burnt. "M. Darchambeau, who was wounded (in the cellar of a burning house), asked a young officer for mercy. This young

* S. pp. 16-18; xvii. p. 56.
† S. p. 18; Mercier.

officer of barely 22, in front of the women and children, aimed his revolver at M. Darchambeau's head and killed him."

The fate of *Pepinster** is recorded in a German diary: "Aug. 12th, Pepinster, Burgomaster, priest, and schoolmaster shot; houses reduced to ashes. March on." As a matter of fact, the three hostages were not shot, but reprieved. The Burgomaster of *Cornesse†* was shot in their stead (a 33, 34)—"an old man and quite deaf. (He was only hit in the leg, and a German officer came up and shot him through the heart with his revolver.)" Five houses in Cornesse were burnt. At *Soiron,‡* on Aug. 4th, the Germans bivouacking there fired on one another, and eight German soldiers were wounded or killed. "But the officers," deposes a German private§ who was present at the scene, "in their anxiety to prevent the fact of this blunder from being reported, hastened to pretend that it was really the civilians who had fired, and gave orders for a general massacre. This order was carried out, and there was terrible butchery. I must mention that we only killed the males, but we burned all the houses." At *Olnes‖* the curé and the communal

---

* Bland p. 185.
† xvii; a 33, 34.
‡ xvii; Reply p. 126.
§ Reply p. 126.
‖ xvii; Mercier; S. pp. 79-82.

secretary were shot on Aug. 5th, and the schoolmaster the same evening, in front of his burning house, with his daughter and his two sons. Only two members of the schoolmaster's family were spared. In the hamlet of *St. Hadelin*,* which came within the radius of Fort Fléron's guns, there was a wholesale massacre on the same date. Early in the day the Germans "requisitioned" 300 bottles of wine; later they drove a crowd of people from St. Hadelin, *Riessonsart*, and *Ayeneux*, to a place called the Faveu, and shot down 33. The remainder were forced to haul German artillery towards the forts, but these were partly released next day, and partly massacred at the Heids d'Olne. Twenty inhabitants of Ayeneux were massacred in a batch elsewhere. Sixty-two civilians were murdered altogether in the commune of Olne, and 78 houses destroyed—40 in St. Hadelin and 38 in Olne itself.

At *Forêt*† the Germans burned a farm and killed two of the farmer's sons on Aug. 5th as they entered the place. They drove the farmer and his two surviving sons in front of them as a screen. The schoolmaster and two others were shot outside the village. "At Forêt," states the German soldier quoted above,‡ "we found prisoners—a priest and five civilians, including a boy of 17. Pillage began . . . but we were shelled . . . and moved off to the next village. The

---

* S. pp. 82-92.
† xvii; S. pp. 92-4.
‡ Reply p. 126.

house doors were at once broken in with the butt-ends of muskets. We pillaged everything. We made piles of the curtains and everything inflammable, and set them alight. All the houses were burnt. It was in the middle of this that the civilian prisoners of whom I have spoken were shot, with the exception of the curé." (The curé, too, was shot that night.)* "A little further on, under the pretext that civilians had fired from a house (though for my own part I cannot say whether they were soldiers or civilians who fired), orders were given to burn the house. A woman asleep there was dragged from her bed, thrown into the flames, and burnt alive. . . ."

Thirteen people in all were killed at Forêt, and 6 houses destroyed. At *Magnée*† 18 houses were destroyed and 21 people killed. The German troops in Magnée were caught by the fire from the Fléron and Chaudfontaine forts, and they revenged themselves, as elsewhere, on the civilians, shooting people in batches and burning houses and farms. This was on Aug. 6th, and at *Romsée*,‡ on the same day, 34 houses were burnt and 31 civilians murdered—some of them being driven as a screen in front of the German troops under the fire of Fort Chaudfontaine.

* Mercier.
† S. pp. 94-100.
‡ S. pp. 100-5.

(vi) *Between the Vesdre and the Ourthe.*

The same outrages were committed between the Vesdre and the Ourthe. At *Louveigné*,* on Aug. 7th, the Germans, retreating from their attack on the southern forts, looted the drink-shops, fired in the streets, and accused the civilians of having shot. A dozen men (two of them over 70 years old) were imprisoned as hostages in a forge, and were shot down, when released, like game in the open. That evening Louveigné was systematically set on fire with the same incendiary apparatus that was used at Visé, and the curé was dragged round on the foot-board of a military motor-car to watch the work. There were more murders next day. The total number of civilians murdered at Louveigné was 29, and there were 77 houses burnt. The devastation impressed the German soldiers who passed through Louveigné on the following days. "Louveigné has been completely burnt out. All the inhabitants are dead," writes a German diarist on Aug. 9th. "March to Louveigné," another records on Aug. 16th. "Several citizens and the curé shot according to martial law, some not yet buried—still lying where they were executed, for everyone to see. Stench of corpses everywhere. Curé said to have incited the inhabitants to ambush and kill the Germans." —"Bivouac! Rain! Burnt villages! Louveigné!"

---

* S. pp. 40-5: Belg. Ann. 5, pp. 167-8; Morgan p. 100; Bryce p. 172.

another exclaims on Aug. 17th. "We marched and bivouacked in the rain, in an orchard with a high hedge round it, full of fruit-trees. There was an abandoned house in front of it. The door, which was locked, was broken in with an axe. The traces of war—burnt houses, weeping women and children, executions of franc-tireurs—showed us the ruthlessness of the times. We could not have done otherwise. . . . But how many have to suffer with others, how many innocent people are shot by martial law, because there is no detailed enquiry first. . . ."

At *Lincé*,* in the commune of Sprimont, a German officer was wounded when the troops returned in confusion from before the southern forts of Liége. The Germans forbade an autopsy to discover by what bullet the wound had been caused, and condemned two civilians with a proven alibi to be shot. All the next morning the destruction went on. Houses were burnt, the curé was mishandled, a farmer and his son were shot down at their farm gate, a girl of twelve received four bullets in her body. The execution of the hostages took place in the afternoon. Sixteen men were shot, of whom 7 were more than 60 years old. At *Chanxhe*,† on Aug. 6th, hostages from *Poulseur* were bound in ranks to the parapet of the bridge over the Ourthe, and kept there several days while the Germans

* S. pp. 30-8.
† S. pp. 20-30.

filed across. "We were tortured by hunger and thirst," writes one of them. "We shivered at night. And then, of necessity, there was the filth. . . . At the end of the bridge the women were pleading with the Germans in vain, and the children were crying." On the 5th two civilian captives were shot on the bridge, and their bodies thrown into the river, and two more (one aged 70) were shot on the 7th. In the commune of Poulseur, from which these hostages came, 7 civilians were killed and 25 houses destroyed. In the commune of Sprimont 67 houses were destroyed and 48 civilians killed. At *Esneux* 26 houses were destroyed and 7 civilians killed.

(vii) *Across the Meuse.*

Meanwhile, the Germans had crossed the Meuse at Visé, and were descending on Liége from the north. At *Hallembaye*, in the commune of *Haccourt*,* 18 people were killed. There were women, children and old men among them, and also the curé,† who was bayonetted on his church threshold as he was removing the sacrament. In the commune of Haccourt 80 houses were destroyed, and 112 hostages were carried away into Germany. *Hermalle-sous-Argenteau*‡ was plundered on Aug. 15th, and 9 houses destroyed. There

---

* S. pp. 191-3; xvii.
† Mercier.
‡ S. pp. 190-1, a 15.

44

was a mock execution of hostages in the presence of women and children, and 368 men of the place were imprisoned in the church for 17 days. At' *Vivegnis** 6 civilians were shot on Aug. 13th, and 45 houses destroyed the day after. The Germans fired on the inhabitants through the windows and doors, and two men were thus killed in a single household. At *Heure-le-Romain†* the population was confined in the church on Aug. 16th (it was Sunday) and compelled to stand there, hands raised, under the muzzle of a machine-gun. Seven civilians were shot at Heure-le-Romain that day, including the Burgomaster's brother and the curé,‡ who were roped together and shot against the church wall. All through the 16th and 17th the sack continued; on the 18th fresh troops arrived and completed the work by systematic arson and the slaughter of 19 people more. Twenty-seven civilians were killed at Heure-le-Romain altogether and 84 houses destroyed. At *Hermée,§* on Aug. 6th, the Germans, caught by the fire of *Fort Pontisse*, revenged themselves by shooting 11 civilians, including old men of 76 and 82 years. On the 14th, the day after the surrender of the fort, the inhabitants of Hermée were driven from their homes and the village systematically burnt, 146 houses out of 308 being destroyed. In the

* S. pp. 187-8.
† S. pp. 200-5; xvii; a 17.
‡ Mercier.
§ S. pp. 194-200; xvii; a 35.

village itself, as apart from the outlying hamlets of the commune, only two or three houses were left standing. At *Fexhe-Slins*, near Hermée, 3 people were killed. Twenty-three were killed, and 13 houses destroyed, in the hamlet of *Rhées* in the commune of *Herstal.**

Thus the Germans plundered private property, burned down houses, and shot civilians of both sexes and all ages, on every road by which they marched upon Liége—from the north-east, the south-east, and the north. One thousand and thirty-two civilians† were shot by the Germans in the whole *Province of Liége*, and 3,173 houses were destroyed in two arrondissements (those of Liége and Verviers) alone out of the four of which the Province is made up.

(viii) *The City of Liége.*

Twenty-nine of these civilians were killed and 55‡ of the houses destroyed in the *city of Liége* itself—on August 20th, a fortnight after it had fallen into the German Army's possession. The Germans entered Liége on August 7th. Their entry was not opposed by Belgian troops, and arms in private hands had already been called in by the Belgian police.§ The Germans

---

* S. pp. 185-7; a 6, 10, 11, 13.

† Known by name. See Reply, p. 142.

‡ There were also thirty-seven houses destroyed in the suburb of Grivegnée.

§ a 24.

found themselves in peaceful occupation of a great industrial city, caught in the full tide of its normal life. There was nothing to suggest outrage, still less to excuse it, in their surroundings there; their conduct on August 20th was deliberate and cold-blooded. The Higher Command was faced with the problem of holding a conquered country, and wanted an example. The troops in garrison were demoralised by the sudden change to idleness from fatigue and danger, and were ready for excitement and pillage.

"Aug. 16th, Liége," writes a German soldier in his diary.* "The villages we passed through had been destroyed.

"Aug. 19th. Quartered in University. Gone on the loose and boozed through the streets of Liége. Lie on straw; enough booze; too little to eat, or we must steal.

"Aug. 20th. In the night the inhabitants of Liége became mutinous. Forty persons were shot and 15 houses demolished. Ten soldiers were shot. The sights here make you cry."

There are proofs of German premeditation—warnings from German soldiers to civilians on whom they were billeted,† and an ammunition waggon which drew up at 8.0 a.m. in the Rue des Pitteurs, and twelve

* Bryce pp. 172-3.
† a 28.

hours later disgorged the benzine with which the houses in that street were drenched before being burnt.*

"The city was perfectly quiet," declares a Belgian witness,† "until about 8.0 p.m. At about 9.15 p.m. I was in bed reading when I heard the sound of rifle-fire. . . . The noise of the firing came nearer and nearer." The first shot was fired from a window of "Emulation Building," looking out on the Place de l'Université, in the heart of the town.‡ The Place was immediately crowded with armed German soldiers, firing in the air, breaking into houses, and dragging out any civilians they could find. First nine men (5 of them Spanish subjects) were shot in a batch, then 7 more.§ "About 10.0 p.m. they were shooting everywhere. About 10.30 p.m. several machine guns were firing and artillery as well." (The artillery was firing on private houses from the opposite side of the Meuse.‖) "About 11.0 p.m. I saw between 45 and 50 houses burning. There were two seats of the fire—the first at the Place de l'Université (8 houses—I was close by at the time), the second across the Meuse on the Quai des Pecheurs, where there were about 35 houses burning. I heard a whole series of orders given in German, and also bugle calls, followed by the cries

* a 24.
† a 28.
‡ S. p. 209.
§ Names given by S. pp. 211-2; cp. a 27.
‖ S. p. 212.

5. Ans: The Church

6. Liège: A Farm House

of the victims, and I saw women with children running about in the street, pursued by soldiers. . . ." (a 28).

The arson was elaborate. In the Rue des Pitteurs the waggon loaded with benzine moved from door to door.* "About 20 men were going up to each of the houses. One of them had a sort of syringe, with which he squirted into the house, and another would throw a bucket of water in. A handful of stuff was first put into the bucket, and when this was thrown into the house there was an immediate explosion" (a 31). At the Place de l'Université, when the Belgian fire-brigade arrived, they were forbidden to extinguish the fire, and made to stand, hands up, against a wall (a 28, 29). Later they were assigned another task. "About midnight," states a witness (a 30), "a whole heap of civilian corpses were brought to the Hôtel de Ville on a fire-brigade cart. There were 17 of them. Bits were blown out of their heads. . . ."

As the houses caught fire the inmates tried to escape. The few who reached the street were shot down (a 24, 26). Most were driven back into the flames. "At about 30 of the houses," a witness states (a 31), "I actually saw faces at the windows before the Germans entered, and then saw the same faces at the cellar windows after the Germans had driven the people into the cellars." In this way a number of men and women

---

* a 24, 27, 31.

were burnt alive.*   In some cases the Germans would
not wait for the fire to do their work for them, but
bayonetted the people themselves.   In one house, near
the Episcopal Palace,† two boys were bayonetted
before their mother's eyes, and then the man—their
father and her husband.   Another man in the house
was wounded almost to death, and the Germans were
with difficulty prevented from "finishing him off,"
next morning, on the way to the hospital.   An orphan
girl, who lodged in the same house, was violated.

Next morning, August 21st, the district round the
University Buildings on either side of the Meuse was
cleared of its inhabitants—such inhabitants as survived and such streets as still stood.   The people were
evicted at a few hours' notice, and not allowed to
return for a month.‡   The same day a proclamation
was posted by the German authorities: "Civilians
have fired on the German soldiers.   Repression is the
result."§   The indictment was not convincing, for
"Emulation Building," from which the first shot was
fired on the night of the 20th, had been cleared of its
Belgian occupants some days before and filled entirely
with German soldiers.   Later the German Governor
of Liége shifted his ground, and laid the blame on
Russian students "who had been a burden on the

---

* a 31; S. p. 213.
† S. pp. 219-224.
‡ S. pp. 217-8, 225.
§ S. p. 218.

population of the city."*   A clearer light is thrown on the outbreak of August 20th by what occurred on the night of August 21st-22nd. "Aug. 22nd, 3 a.m., Liége," writes a German in his diary. "Two infantry regiments shot at each other. Nine dead and 50 wounded—fault not yet ascertained."   But in the other diary, quoted before, the incident is thus recorded under the same date: "August 21st. In the night the soldiers were again fired on. We then destroyed several houses more."   The soldiers fire, the civilians suffer reprisals, but the Germans' object is gained. The conquered population is terrorised, the invaders feel secure. "On August 23rd everything quiet," the latter diarist continues. "The inhabitants have so far given in.

"August 24th. Our occupation is bathing, and eating and drinking for the rest of the day. We live like God in Belgium."

---

* S. p. 234; a 24.

III. FROM LIÉGE TO MALINES.

(i) *Through Limburg to Aerschot.*

The first German force to push forward from Liége was the column commissioned to mask the Belgian fortress of Antwerp on the extreme right flank of the German advance. From the bridges of the Meuse this column marched north-west across the *Province of Limburg.* Belgian patrols met the advance-guard already at *Lanaeken* on August 6th, driving civilians in front of it as a screen.* The invaders were obsessed with the terror of franc-tireurs. At *Hasselt,*† on August 17th, they made the Burgomaster post a proclamation advising his fellow-citizens "to abstain from any kind of provocative demonstration and from all acts of hostility, which might bring terrible reprisals upon our town.

"Above all you must abstain from acts of violence against the German troops, and especially from firing on them.

"In case the inhabitants fire upon the soldiers of the German Army, a third of the male population will be shot."

---

* xv p. 20.
† Bryce pp. 183-4.

7. Liège Under German Occupation

8. Liège Under the Germans: Ruins and Placards

At *Tongres*,* on August 18th, the Germans carried threats into action. The population was driven out bodily from the town, and the town systematically plundered. At least 17 civilians were killed (including a boy of 12), and a number of houses were burnt. "On August 18th," writes a German in his diary, "we reach Tongres. Here, too, it is a complete picture of destruction—something unique of its kind for our profession."†—"Tongres," writes another on the 19th. "A quantity of houses plundered by our cavalry." A captured letter from the hand of a German army-doctor reveals the pretext on which this was done. "The Belgians have only themselves to thank that their country has been devastated in this way. I have seen all the great towns attacked and the villages besieged and set on fire. At Tongres we were attacked by the population in the evening *when it was dark*. An immense number of shots were exchanged, for we were exposed to fire on four sides. *Happily we had only one man hit*—he died the following day. We killed two women, and the men were shot the day after." There is no disproof here of the Belgian affirmation that the shots were fired by the Germans themselves.

This outbreak at Tongres on August 18th was not an isolated occurrence. On the same day the Germans

---

*xvii p. 66; xxi p. 129; Morgan p. 101; Bland p. 121; Davignon p. 107.
† The man was a glass-maker.

shot down the Burgomaster's wife and a lawyer at *Cannes*,* and two men and a boy at *Lixht*,† a few miles north-west of the Visé bridge. But Limburg suffered little compared to Brabant, into which the Germans next advanced.

Haelen, where their advance-guard was severely handled by the Belgian Army on August 12th, lies close to the boundary between the two provinces, and they took vengeance on the civil population of *Brabant* for this military reverse.

"The Germans came to *Schaffen*,"‡ the curé reports, "at 9.0 o'clock on August 18th. They set fire to 170 houses. A thousand inhabitants are homeless. The communal building and my own residence are among the houses burnt. Twenty-two people at least were killed without motive. Two men (mentioned by name) were buried alive head downwards, in the presence of their wives. The Germans seized me in my garden, and mishandled me in every kind of way. . . . The blacksmith, who was a prisoner with me, had his arm broken and was then killed. . . . It went on all day long.. Towards evening they made me look at the church, saying it was the last time I should see it. About 6.45 they let me go. I was bleeding and uncon-

---

* xvii p. 66.
† xvii p. 63.
‡ Reply pp. 140-1; k4; Bédier pp. 10-1; i pp. 3-4.

scious. An officer made me get up and bade me be off. At several metres distance they fired on me. I fell down and was left for dead. It was my salvation. . . .

"All the houses were drenched, before burning, with naphtha and petrol, which the Germans carry with them. . . ."

On the German side, there is the ordinary excuse. "Fifty civilians," writes a diarist, "had hidden in the church tower and had fired on our men with a machine-gun.* All the civilians were shot."

The curé mentions that the Germans found the church door locked, broke it in, and then found no one there.

At *Molenstede*, another village in the *Canton of Diest*, 32 houses were burnt and 11 civilians killed. In the whole Canton 226 houses were burnt, and 47 people killed in all.

The Germans were also advancing by a more southerly road from Tongres through St. Trond. At *St. Trond*,† the first Uhlans killed 2 civilians in the street and wounded others. At *Budirgen* they killed 2 civilians and burned 58 houses, at *Neerlinter* one and 73. In the *Canton of Léau* they killed 19 civilians altogether, and 174 houses were destroyed.

---

* There had been Belgian *soldiers* with a machine-gun in the village.

† k18.

... n the Canton of Tirlemont, they
... burned 32 houses and pillaged 150
... At *Tirlemont* itself, they killed
... and burned 60 houses. At *Hougaerde*,*
... ered the village, they drove the curé of
... before them as a screen, and he was killed
... bullet from the Belgian troops, who were
... the road from behind a barricade. Four
... were killed at Hougaerde, 100 houses pil-
... and 40 destroyed. In the whole *Canton of*
... the Germans killed 18 civilians, and burned
... down.

... they killed 4 people and burned 20
... at *Roosbeek* 3 and 42. "After Roosbeek," a
... diarist notes,† "we began to have an idea of
... houses burnt, walls pierced by bullets, the
... of the tower carried away by shells, and so on. A
... isolated crosses marked the graves of the victims."
... ‡ the Germans used civilians as a screen
... and killed two more when they entered the vil-
... At *Lovenjoul* they killed 6 civilians and burned
... houses, at *Lubbeek* 15 and 46. In the *Canton of*
... 16 civilians were killed from first to last,
... 170 houses destroyed.

* Kroll p. 108
† Passman p. 90
‡ xx p. 80

56

(ii) *Aerschot.*

The Germans marched into *Aerschot** on the morning of Aug. 19th, driving before them two girls and four women with babies in their arms as a screen.† One of the women was wounded by the fire of the Belgian troops, who had posted machine guns to dispute the Germans' entry, but now withheld their fire and retired from the town. The Germans encountered no further resistance, but they began to kill civilians and break into houses immediately they came in. They bayonetted two women on their doorstep (c 27). They shot a deaf boy (c 1) who did not understand the order to raise his hands. They shot 5 men they had requisitioned as guides (R. No. 3). They fired at the church (c 18). They fired at people looking out of the windows of their houses (R. No. 5). The Burgomaster's son, a boy of fifteen, was standing at a window with his mother and was wounded by a bullet in the leg (R. No. 11). They killed people in their houses. Six men, for instance, were bayonetted in one house (R. No. 15). They dragged a railway employé from his home and shot him in a field (R. No. 2). "I went back home," states a woman who had been seized by the Germans and had escaped (c 18), "and found my husband lying dead outside it. He had been

---

* c1-38; Belg. xxi pp. 111-4; Anns. 1, 7; Reply pp. 147-178; German White Book, A; Struycken; Davignon p. 97.

† Reply No. 1; g2.

shot through the head from behind. His pockets had been rifled."

Other civilians (the civil population was already accused of having fired) were collected as hostages,* and driven, with their hands raised above their heads, to an open space on the banks of the River Démer. "There were about 200 prisoners, some of them invalids taken from their beds" (c 1). There was a professor from the College among them (R. No. 9), and an old man of 75 (c 15). After these hostages had been searched, and had been kept standing by the river, with their arms up, for two hours, the Burgomaster was brought to them under guard,† and compelled to read out a proclamation, ordering all arms to be given up, and warning that if a shot were fired by a civilian, the man who fired it, and four others with him, would be put to death. It was a gratuitous proceeding, for, several days before the Germans arrived, the Burgomaster (like most of his colleagues throughout Belgium) had sent the town crier round, calling on the population to deposit all arms at the Hôtel-de-Ville, and he had posted placards on the walls to the same effect (c 4, 7). A priest drew a German officer's attention to these placards (c 20), and the Burgomaster himself had already given a translation of their contents to the German commandant

---

* c1, 6, 9, 15; R. No. 9.
† c1, 15; R. Nos. 4, 9, 11.

(R. No. 11). That officer* disingenuously represents this act of good faith as a suspicious circumstance. "To my special surprise," he states, "thirty-six more rifles, professedly intended for public processions and for the Garde Civique, were produced" (from the Hôtel-de-Ville). "The constituents of ammunition for these rifles were also found packed in a case." But the only weapon still found in private hands on the morning of Aug. 19th was a shot gun used for pigeon shooting (c 1), and when the owner had fetched it from his home the hostages were released. Yet at this point 4 more civilians were shot down, two of them father and son—the son feeble-minded (c 15).

The Germans quartered in Aerschot were already getting out of hand. "I saw the dead body of another man in the street," continues the witness (c 15) quoted above. "When I got to my house, I found that all the furniture had been broken, and that the place had been thoroughly ransacked, and everything of value stolen. When I came out into the street again I saw the dead body of a man at the door of the next house to mine. He was my neighbour, and wore a Red Cross brassard on his arm. . . ."

The Germans gave themselves up to drink and plunder. "They set about breaking in the cellar doors, and soon most of them were drunk" (R. No. 15).— "An officer came to me," states another witness (c 7),

---

* German White Book, A 2.

"and demanded a packet of coffee. He did not pay for it. He gave no receipt."—"They broke my shop window," deposes another. "The shop front was pillaged in a moment. Then they gutted the shop itself. They fought each other for the bottles of cognac and rum. In the middle of this an officer entered. He did not seem at all surprised, and demanded three bottles of cognac and three of wine for himself. The soldiers, N.C.O.'s and officers, went down to the cellar and emptied it. . . ." Not even the Red Cross was spared. The monastery of St. Damien, which had been turned into an ambulance, was broken into by German soldiers, who accused the monks of firing and tore the bandages off the wounded Belgian soldiers to make sure that the wounds were real (R. No. 16). "Whenever we referred to our membership of the Red Cross," declares one of the monks, "our words were received with scornful smiles and comments, indicating clearly that they made no account of that."

About 5.0 p.m. Colonel Stenger, the commander of the 8th German Infantry Brigade, arrived in Aerschot with his staff. They were quartered in the Burgomaster's house, in rooms overlooking the square. Captain Karge, the commander of the divisional military police, was billeted on the Burgomaster's brother, also in the square but on the opposite side. About 8.0 p.m. (German time) Colonel Stenger was standing on the Burgomaster's balcony; the Burgomaster, who had just

60

9. LIÈGE IN RUINS

10. "We Live Like God in Belgium"

been allowed to return home, was at his front door, offering the German sentries cigars, and his wife was close by him; the square was full of troops, and a supply column was just filing through, when suddenly a single loud shot was fired, followed immediately by a heavy fusillade. "I very distinctly saw two columns of smoke," writes the Burgomaster's wife (R. No. 11), "followed by a multitude of discharges."—"I could perceive a light cloud of smoke and dust," states Captain Karge,* who was at his window across the square, "coming from the eaves of a red corner house." In a moment the soldiers massed in the square were in an uproar. "My yard," continues the Burgomaster's wife, "was immediately invaded by horses and by soldiers firing in the air like madmen."—"The drivers and transport men," observes Captain Karge, "had left their horses and waggons and taken cover from the shots in the entrances of the houses. Some of the waggons had interlocked, because the horses, becoming restless, had taken their own course without the drivers to guide them." Another German officer † thought the firing came from the north-west outskirts of the town, and was told by fugitive German soldiers that there were Belgian troops advancing to the attack. A machine-gun company went out to meet them, and marched three kilometres before it discovered that there

* White Book A 3, Appendix.
† White Book A 5.

was no enemy, and turned back. "About 350 yards from the square," states the commander of this unit,* "I met cavalry dashing backwards and transport waggons trying to turn round. . . . I saw shots coming from the houses, whereupon I ordered the machine guns to be unlimbered and the house fronts on the left to be fired upon."

Who fired the first shot? Who fired the answering volley? There is abundant evidence, both Belgian and German, of German soldiers firing in the square and the neighbouring streets; no single instance is proved, or even alleged, in the German White Book, of a Belgian caught in the act of firing. "The situation developed," deposes Captain Folz,† "into our men pressing their backs against the houses, and firing on any marksman in the opposite house, as soon as he showed himself." But were they Belgians at the windows, or Germans taking cover from the undoubted fire of their comrades, and replying from these vantage points upon an imaginary foe? "Near the Hôtel-de-Ville," continues Captain Folz, "there stood an officer who had the signal 'Cease Fire' blown continuously.‡ Clearly this officer desired in the first place to stop the shooting of our men, in order to set a systematic action on foot."

* A 4.
† White Book A 5.
‡ cp. A 3, Appendix.

The German soldiers' minds had been filled with lying rumours. "I heard," declares Captain **Karge**, "that the King of the Belgians had decreed that every male Belgian was under obligation to do the German Army as much harm as possible. . . .

"An officer told me he had read on a church .door that the Belgians were forbidden to hold captured German officers on parole, but had to shoot them. . . .

"A seminary teacher assured me" (it was under the threat of death) "definitely, as I now think that I can distinctly remember, that the Garde Civique had been ordered to injure the German Army in every possible way. . . ."

Thus, when he heard the shots, Captain Karge leapt to his conclusions. "The regularity of the volleys gave me the impression that the affair was well organised and possibly under military command." It never occurred to him that they might be German volleys commanded by German officers as apprehensive as himself. "Everywhere, apparently," he proceeds, "the firing came, *not from the windows*, but from roof-openings or prepared loopholes in the attics of the houses." But if not from the windows, why not from the square, which was crowded with German soldiers, when a moment afterwards (admittedly) these very soldiers were firing furiously? "This" (assumed direction from which the firing came) "is the explanation of the smallness of the damage done by the shots to men and animals," and, in fact, the only victim the Germans claim is Colonel Stenger, the Brigadier. After the worst firing was over and the troops were getting under control, Colonel Stenger was found by his aide-de-camp (A 2), who had come up to his room to make a report, lying wounded on the floor and on the point of death. Captain Folz (A 5) records that "the Regimental Surgeon of the Infantry Regiment No. 140, who made a post-mortem examination of the body in his presence on the following day, found in the aperture of the breast wound a deformed leaden bullet, which had been shattered by contact with a hard object." It remains to prove that the bullet was not German. The German White Book does not include any report from the examining surgeon himself.

Meanwhile, the town and people of Aerschot were given over to destruction. "I now took some soldiers," proceeds Captain Karge, "and went with them towards the house from which the shooting"—in Captain Karge's belief—"had first come. . . . I ordered the doors and windows of the ground floor, which were securely locked, to be broken in. Thereupon I pushed into the house with the others, and using a fairly large quantity of turpentine, which was found in a can of about 20 litres capacity, and which I had poured out partly on the first storey and then down the stairs and on the ground floor, succeeded in setting the house on fire in a very short time. Further, I had ordered the

II. HAELEN

12. AERSCHOT

men not taking part in this to guard the entrances of the house and arrest all male persons escaping from it. When I left the burning house several civilians, including a young priest, had been arrested from the *adjoining* houses. 'I had these brought to the square, where in the meantime my company of military police had collected.

"I then . . . took command of all prisoners, among whom I set free the women, boys and girls. I was ordered by a staff officer to shoot the prisoners. Then I ordered my police . . . to escort the prisoners and take them out of the town. Here, at the exit, a house was burning, and by the light of it I had the culprits—88 in number, after I had separated out three cripples—shot. . . ."

These 88 victims were only a preliminary batch. The whole population of Aerschot was being hunted out of the houses by the German troops and driven together into the square. They were driven along with brutal violence. "One of the Germans thrust at me with his bayonet," states one woman (c 9), "which passed through my skirt and behind my knees. I was too frightened to notice much."—"When we got into the street," states another (c 10), "other German soldiers fired at us. I was carrying a child in my arms, and a bullet passed through my left hand and my child's left arm. The child was also hit on the fundament. , , , In the hospital, on Aug. 22nd, I saw three women die of wounds."—"In the ambulance at the Institut Damien," reports the monk quoted above, "we nursed four women, several civilians and some children. A one-year-old child had received a bayonet wound in its thigh while its mother was carrying it in her arms. Several civilians had burns on their bodies and bullet wounds as well. They told us how the soldiers set fire to the houses and fired on the suffocating inhabitants when they tried to escape."

As elsewhere, the incendiarism was systematic. "They used a special apparatus, something like a big rifle, for throwing naphtha or some similar inflammable substance" (c 19).—"I was taken to the officer in command," states a professor (c 14). "I found him personally assisting in setting fire to a house. He and his men were lighting matches and setting them to the curtains."—"We saw a whole street burning, in which I possessed two houses," deposes a native of Aerschot, who was being driven towards the square. "We heard children and beasts crying in the flames" (c 2). A civilian went out into the street to see if his mother was in a burning house. He was shot down by Germans at a distance of 18 yards (c 5). Another householder (R. No. 5) threw his child out of the first-floor window of his burning house, jumped out himself, and broke both his legs. His wife was burnt alive. "The Germans with their rifles prevented anyone going to help this man, and he had to drag himself along with his legs broken as best he could" (c 19).—"The whole upper part of my house caught fire," declares another (R. No. 13), "when there were a dozen people in it. The Germans had blocked the street door to prevent them coming out. They tried in vain to reach the neighbouring roofs. . . . The Germans were firing on everyone in the streets. . . ."

By this time the Germans were mostly drunk (c9) and lost to all reason or shame. Two men and a boy stepped out of the door of a public-house in which they had taken refuge with others. "As soon as we got outside we saw the flash of rifles and heard the report. . . . We came in as quickly as we could and shut the door. The German soldiers entered. The first man who entered said, 'You have been shooting,' and the others kept repeating the same words. They pointed their revolvers at us, and threatened to shoot us if we moved" (c 4).

In another building about 22 captured Belgian soldiers (some of them wounded) and six civilian hostages were under guard. They were dragged out to the banks of the Démer and shot down by two companies of German troops. "I was hit," explains one of the two survivors (a soldier already wounded before being taken prisoner), "but an officer saw that I was still breathing, and when a soldier wanted to shoot me again, he ordered him to throw me into the Démer. I clung to a branch and set my feet against the stones on the river-bottom. I stayed there till the following morning, with only my head above water. . . ." (R. No. 8).

The Burgomaster's house was the first to be cleared. Colonel Stenger's aide-de-camp dragged the Burgomaster out of the cellar where he and his family had taken refuge, and carried him off under guard. Half-an-hour later the aide-de-camp returned for the Burgomaster's wife and his fifteen-year-old son. "My poor child," writes the Burgomaster's wife, "could scarcely walk because of his wound. The aide-de-camp kicked him along. I shut my eyes to see no more. . . ." (R. No. 11).

"When we reached the square," the same witness continues, "we found there all our neighbours. A girl near me was fainting with grief. Her father and two brothers had been shot, and they had torn her from her dying mother's bedside. (They found her, nine hours later, dead). All the houses on the right side of the square were ablaze. One could detect the perfect order and method with which they were proceeding. There was none of the feverishness of men left to pillage by themselves. I am positive they were acting with orderliness and under orders. . . . From time to time, soldiers emerged from our house, with their arms full of bottles of wine. They were opening our windows, and all the interiors were stripped bare. . . ."—"The square was one blaze of fire," states a blacksmith (c 1), "and the civilians were obliged to stand there close to the flames from the burning houses."—"They put the women and children on one side," adds a woman (c 7). "I was among them, and my 5 children—one boy of fifteen and 4 girls. I saw that many of the men had their hands tied. They took the men away along the road to Louvain. . . ."

The men were being led out of the town, as Captain Karge's prisoners had been led out a few hours before, to be shot. The Burgomaster, his brother, and his son were in this second convoy. "Under the glare of the conflagration," writes the Burgomaster's wife, "my eyes fell upon my husband, my son and my brother-in-law, who were being led, with other men, to execution. For fear of breaking down his courage, I could not even cry out to my husband: 'I am here.'" There were 50 or 60 prisoners altogether, and another batch of 30 followed behind.* "They made us walk in the same position, hands up, for 20 minutes," one survivor states (c 4). "When we got tired we put our hands on our heads."—"One of the prisoners," states a second member of the convoy (c 8), "was struck on the back with a rifle-butt by a German soldier. The young man said: 'O my father.' His father said: 'Keep quiet, my boy.' Another soldier thrust his bayonet into the thigh of another prisoner, and afterwards compelled him to walk on with the rest."—"Our hands,"

---

* c 4, 8.

states a third (R. No. 7), "were bound behind our backs with copper wire—so tightly that our wrists were cut and bled. We were compelled to lie down, still bound, on our backs, with our heads touching the ground. About six in the morning, they decided to begin the executions."

An officer read out a document to the prisoners.— One out of three was to be shot. "It was read out like an article of the law. He read in German, but we understood it. . . . They took all the young men. . . ." (c 4).

The Burgomaster's chief political opponent was among the prisoners. He offered his life for the Burgomaster's—"The Burgomaster's life was essential to the welfare of the town." The Burgomaster pleaded for his fellow citizens, and then for his son. The officer answered that he must have them all—the Burgomaster, his son and his brother. "The boy got up and stood between his father and uncle. . . . The shots rang out, and the three bodies fell heavily one upon another . . ." (R. No. 7).

"The rest were drawn up in ranks of three. They numbered them—one, two, three. Each number three had to step out of his rank and fall in behind the corpses; they were going to be shot, the Germans said. My brother and I were next to each other—I number two, he three. I asked the officer if I might take my brother's place: 'My mother is a widow. My brother has finished his education, and is more useful than I!' The officer was again implacable. 'Step out, number three.' We embraced, and my brother joined the rest. There were about 30 of them lined up. Then the German soldiers moved slowly along the line, killing three at every discharge—each time at the officer's word of command" (R. No. 7).

The last man in the line was spared as a medical student and member of the Red Cross (R. No. 5). The survivors were set free. On their way back they passed another batch going to their death (R. No. 7). They passed the corpse of a woman on the road, and another in the cattle-market (c 17). Other inhabitants of Aerschot were forced to bury all the corpses on the Louvain road in the course of the same day. They brought back to the women of Aerschot the sure knowledge that their husbands, sons and brothers were dead.*

The rest of what happened at Aerschot is quickly told. When the Germans had marched the second convoy of men out of the town and dismissed the women from the square, they evacuated the town themselves† and bombarded it from outside with artillery;‡ but in the daylight of Aug. 20th they came back again, and burned and pillaged continuously for three days

---

* R. No. 3; c 12.
† White Book A 2 and 3 (Appendix).
‡ c 1, 4, 5; R. No. 11.

—taking not only food and clothing but valuables of every kind, and loading them methodically on waggons and motor cars.* On the evening of the 20th, the Institut Damien, hospital though it was, was compelled to provide quarters for 1,100 men. "We spent all night giving food and drink to this mob, of whom many were drunk. We collected 800 empty bottles next morning."†

On Aug. 26th and 27th the remnant of the population—about 600 men, women, and children, who had not perished or fled—were herded into the church.‡ They were given little food, and no means of sanitation. On the evening of the 27th a squad of German soldiers amused themselves by firing through the church door over the heads of the hostages, against the opposite wall. On the 28th the monks of St. Damien were brought there also. (Their hospital was closed, and the patients turned out of their beds.) The rest of the hostages were marched that day to Louvain. There were little children among them, and women with child, and men too old to walk. At Louvain, in the Place de la Station, they were fired upon, and a number were wounded and killed. The survivors were released on the 29th, but when they returned to Aerschot they were arrested and imprisoned

* R. Nos. 9, 10, 15.
† R. No. 16.
‡ c 7, 13, 20, 23-5; R. Nos. 12, 13, 15, 16.

again—the men in the church, the women in a chateau. The women and children were released the day following (that day the active troops at Aerschot were replaced by a landsturm garrison, who began to pillage the town once more).* The men were kept prisoners till Sept. 6th, when those not of military age were released and the remainder (about 70) deported by train to Germany. All the monks were deported, whatever their age.†

"On Aug. 31st," writes a German landsturmer in his diary,‡ "we entered Aerschot to guard the station. On Sept. 2nd I had a little time off duty, which I spent in visiting the town. No one, without seeing it, could form any idea of the condition it is in. . . . In all my life I shall never drink more wine than I drank here."

Three hundred and eighty-six houses were burnt at Aerschot, 1,000 plundered, 150 inhabitants killed, and after this destruction the Germans admitted the innocence of their victims. "It was a beastly mess," a German non-commissioned officer confessed to one of the monks in the church of Aerschot on Aug. 29th.§ "It was our soldiers who fired, but they have been punished."

---

* R. No. 9.
† cp. the treatment of the monks at Louvain, p. 137 below.
‡ Davignon, p. 97.
§ R. p. 171.

(iii) *The Aerschot District.*

The smaller places round Aerschot suffered in their degree. At *Nieuw-Rhode* 200 houses (out of 321) were plundered, one civilian killed, and 27 deported to Germany. At *Gelrode*,* on August 19th, the Germans seized 21 civilians as hostages, imprisoned them in the church, and then shot one in every three against a wall—the rest were marched to Louvain and imprisoned in the church there. None of them were discovered with arms, for the Burgomaster of Gelrode had collected all arms in private hands before the Germans arrived. The priest of Gelrode† was dragged away to Aerschot on August 27th by German soldiers. "When they got to the churchyard the priest was struck several times by each soldier on the head. Then they pushed him against the wall of the church" (c24).—"His hands were raised above his head. Five or six soldiers stood immediately in front of him. . . . When he let his hands drop a little, soldiers brought down their rifle butts on his feet" (c25). Finally they led him away to be shot, and his corpse was thrown into the Démer.

Eighteen civilians altogether were shot in the commune of Gelrode, and 99 deported to Germany. Twenty-three houses were burnt, and 131 plundered, out of 201 in the village.

---

* c39-45.
† c3, 23-5, 40; R. No. 10 (Aerschot).

At *Tremeloo** 214 houses were burnt and 3 civilians
killed (one of them an old man of 72). A number of
women were raped at Tremeloo.

At *Rotselaer*† 67 houses were burnt, 38 civilians
killed, and 120 deported to Germany. A girl who
was raped by five Germans went out of her mind
(c52). The priest of Rotselaer was deported with his
parishioners. The men of the village had been confined in the church on the night of August 22nd, again
on the night of the 23rd, and then consecutively till the
morning of the 27th. The priest of Herent (who was
more than 70 years old)‡ and other men from Herent,
Wackerzeel, and Thildonck, were imprisoned with
them, till there were a thousand people in the church
altogether. The women brought them what food
could be found, but for five days they could neither
wash nor sleep. On the 27th they were marched to
Louvain with a batch of prisoners taken from Louvain itself, and were sent on the terrible journey in
cattle-trucks to Aix-la-Chapelle.

At *Wespelaer*§ the destruction was complete. Out
of 297 houses 47 were burnt and 250 gutted. Twenty-
one inhabitants were killed. "The Germans shot the
owner of the first house burnt on his doorstep, and his
twenty-years-old daughter inside. . . . I only saw one

---

* c54-6.
† c48-9, 52; R. pp. 351-3.
‡ For his death see footnote on p. 151 below.
§ c60-63.

man shot with my own eyes—a man who had an old carbine in his house. It had not been used; he was not carrying it. . . . In another house a married couple, 80 years old, were burnt alive". (c60).

At *Campenhout** the Germans burned 85 houses and killed 14 civilians. In a rich man's house, where officers were quartered, they rifled the wine cellar and shot the mistress of the house in cold blood as she entered the room where they were drinking. "The other officers continued to drink and sing, and did not pay great attention to the killing of my mistress," states a servant who was present. As they continued their advance, the Germans collected about 400 men, women and children (some of the women with babies in their arms) from Campenhout, Elewyt and Malines, and drove them forward as a screen, with the priest of Campenhout at their head, against the Belgian forces holding the outer ring of the Antwerp lines.†

The devastation of this district is described by a witness who walked through it, from Brussels to Aerschot, after the Germans had passed (c 25). "We traversed the village of Werchter, where there had been no battle, but it had been in the occupation of the Germans, and on all sides of this village we saw burnt-down houses and traces of plunder and havoc. In Wespelaer and Rotselaer and Wesemael we saw

---

* c 46-47.
† g 16-18.

the same. We did not pass through the village of Gelrode, but close to it, and we saw that houses had been burnt down there. In Aerschot the Malines Street, Hamer Street, Théophile Becker Street and other streets were completely burnt. Half the Grand Place had been burnt down. . . ."

(iv) *The Retreat from Malines.*

Yet the devastation done by the Germans in their advance was light compared with the outrages they committed when the Belgian sortie of August 25th drove them back from Malines towards the Aerschot-Louvain line.

In *Malines* itself* they destroyed 1,500 houses from first to last, and revenged themselves atrociously on the civil population. A Belgian soldier saw them bayonet an old woman in the back, and cut off a young woman's breasts (d 1). Another saw them bayonet a woman and her son (d 2). They shot a police inspector in the stomach as he came out of his door, and blew off the head of an old woman at a window (d 3). A child of two came out into the street as eight drunken soldiers were marching by. "A man in the second file stepped aside and drove his bayonet with both hands into the child's stomach. He lifted the child into the air on his bayonet and carried it away, he and his comrades still singing. The child screamed when the

---

*d 1-9.

soldier struck it with his bayonet, but not afterwards. This incident is reported by two witnesses (d 4-5). Another woman was found dead with twelve bayonet wounds between her shoulders and her waist (d 7). Another—between 16 and 20 years old—who had been killed by a bayonet, "was kneeling, and her hands were clasped, and the bayonet had pierced both hands. I also saw a boy of about 16," continues the witness, "who had been killed by a bayonet thrust through his mouth." In the same house there was an old woman lying dead (d 9).

The next place from which the Germans were driven was *Hofstade*,* and here, too, they revenged themselves before they went. They left the corpses of women lying in the streets. There was an old woman mutilated with the bayonet.† There was a young pregnant woman who had been ripped open.‡ In the lodge of a chateau the porter's body was found lying on a heap of straw.§ He had been bayonetted in the stomach—evidently while in bed, for the empty bed was soaked with blood. The blacksmith of Hofstade —also bayonetted in the stomach—was lying on his doorstep.‖ Adjoining the blacksmith's house there was a café, and here a middle-aged woman lay dead,

* d 10-65; vii p. 54.
† d 18, 20, 21, 34, 52, 62.
‡ d 11, 18, 20, 21, 37, 39, 41, 44.
§ d 36, 38, 40.
‖ d 32-4, 38-9.

and a boy of about 16. The boy was found kneeling in an attitude of supplication. Both his hands had been cut off. "One was on the ground, the other hanging by a bit of skin" (d 25). His face was smeared with blood. He was seen in this condition by twenty-five separate witnesses, whose testimony is recorded in the Bryce Report.* Several saw him before he was quite dead.

In one house at Hofstade† the Belgian troops found the dead bodies of two women and a man. One of the women, who was middle-aged, had been bayonetted in the stomach; the other, who was about 20 years old, had been bayonetted in the head, and her legs had been almost severed from her body. The man had been bayonetted through the head. In another room the body of a ten-year-old boy was suspended from a hanging lamp. He had been killed first by a bayonet wound in the stomach.

"I went with an artilleryman," states another Belgian soldier,‡ "to find his parents who lived in Hofstade. All the houses were burning except the one where this man's parents lived. On forcing the door, we saw lying on the floor of the room on which it opened the dead bodies of a man, a woman, a girl, and a boy, who, the artilleryman told us, were his father

---

* d 12, 13, 16, 17, 20, 21, 25, 27, 29-31, 33, 35, 38, 43, 46, 52, 54-7, 62-5.

† d 10, 13, 15, 26, 47.

‡ d 36, cp. 37.

and mother and brother and sister. Each of them had both feet cut off just above the ankle, and both hands just above the wrist. The poor boy rushed straight off, took one of the horses from his gun, and rode in the direction of the German lines. We never saw him again. . . ."

Retreating from Hofstade, the Germans drove about 200 of the inhabitants with them as a screen, to cover their flank against the Belgian attack.* At *Muysen* they killed 6 civilians and burned 450 houses. "There were broken wine bottles lying about everywhere" (d 88).

At *Sempst*,† as they evacuated the village, they dragged the inhabitants out of their houses. One old man who expostulated was shot by an officer with a revolver,‡ and his son was shot when he attempted to escape. They fired down into the cellars and up through the ceilings to drive the people out (d 68). The hostages were taken to the bridge. "One young man was carrying in his arms his little brother, 10 or 11 years old, who had been run over before the war and could not walk. The soldiers told the man to hold up his arms. He said he could not, as he must hold his brother, who could not walk. Then a German

---

* vii p. 54.
† d 66-83.
‡ d 67-9, 72, 75.

13. BRUSSELS: A BOOKING-OFFICE

14. Malines After Bombardment

soldier hit him on the head with a revolver, and he let the child fall. . . ."

In one house they bound a bed-ridden man to his bed, and shot another man in the presence of 13 children who were in the house (d 29). In another house they burned a woman and two children (d 71); they burned the owner of a bicycle shop in his shop;* these four bodies were found, carbonised, by the Belgian troops. The Belgians also found a woman dead in the street, with four bayonet wounds in her body (d 36), and saw an Uhlan overtake a woman driving in a cart, thrust his lance through her body, and then shoot her in the chest with his carbine (d 80). In a farmhouse the farmer was found with his head cut off. His two sons, killed by bullet wounds, were lying beside him. His wife, whose left breast had been cut off, was still alive, and told how, when her eight-year-old son had gone up a ladder into the loft, the Germans had pulled away the ladder and set the building on fire.† Twenty-seven houses were burnt at Sempst, 200 sacked, 18 inhabitants killed, and 34 deported to Germany.

At *Weerde* 34 houses were burnt. As the Germans retreated they bayonetted two little girls standing in the road and tossed them into the flames of a burning house—their mother was standing by (d 85). At

---

* d 66, 69-72, 77-9.
† d 74, cp. 81.

*Eppeghem** 176 houses were burnt, 8 civilians killed, and 125 deported. The killing was done with the bayonet. A woman with child, whose stomach had been slashed open, died in the hospital at Malines. When the Germans returned to Eppeghem again, they used the remaining civilians as a screen. On August 28th they did the same at *Elewyt,*† not even exempting old men or women with child. We have the testimony of a Belgian priest who was driven in the screen, and of a Belgian soldier in the trenches against which the screen was driven. A hundred and thirty-three houses were burnt at Elewyt, and 10 civilians killed. The Belgian troops found the body of a man tied naked to a ring in a wall. His head was riddled with bullets, there was a bayonet wound in his chest, and he had been mutilated obscenely. A woman, also mutilated obscenely after violation, was lying dead on the ground. In another house a man and a woman were found, with bayonet wounds all over their bodies, on the floor. At *Perck* 180 houses (out of 243) were sacked and 5 civilians killed. At *Bueken* 50 houses were burnt, 30 sacked (out of 84), and 8 civilians killed. The victims were killed in a meadow in the sight of the women and children.‡ Among them was

* d 87-9; g 20.
† xv p. 22; g 18; d 90-1, 26.
‡ x pp. 78-9.

the parish priest.* "He was a man 75 or 80 years old. He could not walk fast enough. He was driven along with blows from rifle-butts and knocked down. He cried out: 'I can go no further,' and a soldier thrust a bayonet into his neck at the back—the blood flowed out in quantities. The old man begged to be shot, but the officer said: 'That is too good for you.' He was taken off behind a house and we heard shots. He did not return. . . ." (d 97, cp. 98). At *Vilvorde*† 33 houses were burnt and 6 civilians killed. In the whole *Canton of Vilvorde*, in which all these places, except Malines, lay, 611 houses were burnt, 1,665 plundered, 90 civilians killed, and 177 deported to Germany.

The devastation spread through the whole zone of the German retreat. At *Capelle-au-Bois*‡ the Belgian troops found two girls hanging naked from a tree with their breasts cut off, and two women bayonetted in a house, caught as they were making preparations to flee. A woman told them how German soldiers had held her down by force, while other soldiers had violated her daughter successively in an adjoining room. Four civilians were killed at Capelle-au-Bois and 235 houses burnt. At *Londerzeel*§ 18 houses were burnt and one civilian killed. He was a man who had tried to pre-

* Mercier.
† d 92-3.
‡ d 112-4; cp. Massart, pp. 338-9.
§ g 22.

vent the Germans from violating his two daughters. When the Germans re-entered Londerzeel they used the civilian population as a screen. At *Ramsdonck*, near Londerzeel, a woman and two children were shot by the Germans as they were flying for protection towards the Belgian lines.* At *Wolverthem* 10 houses were burnt and 5 people killed. At *Meysse* 3 houses were burnt and 350 sacked, 2 civilians killed and 29 deported. At *Beyghem* 32 houses were burnt. At *Pont-Brûlé*,† on Aug. 25th, the priest was imprisoned with 28 other civilian hostages in a room. The German soldiers compelled him to hold up his hands for hours, and struck him when he lowered them from fatigue. They compelled his fellow-prisoners to spit on him. They tore up his breviary and threw the fragments in his face. When he fainted they threw pails of water on him to revive him. As he was reviving he was shot. Fifty-eight houses were burnt in the commune of Pont-Brûlé-Grimbergen, 5 civilians shot, and 65 deported. These places lay in the *Canton of Wolverthem*, west of the river Senne, between Termonde, Malines, and Brussels. In the whole canton 426 houses were burnt, 1,292 plundered, 29 civilians killed, and 182 deported to Germany.

In the district between Malines and Aerschot it was the same, and places which had suffered already on

---

* k 21.
† Reply p. 431; Mercier.

15. Malines : Ruins

16. MALINES: RUINS

Aug. 19th were devastated again on Aug. 25th and the following days. At *Hever** in the Canton of Haecht, a baby was found hanged by the neck to the handle of a door. Thirty-five houses were burnt. At *Boortmeerbeek*† 103 houses were burnt and 300 sacked (out of 437); 5 civilians were killed—one of them a little girl who was bayonetted in the road. At *Haecht*‡ 5 men were seized as hostages and then shot in cold blood. One of them survived, though he was bayonetted twice after the shooting to "finish him off." Seven others were stripped naked and threatened with bayonets, but instead of being killed they were used as a screen. The Belgian troops found the body of a woman on the road, stripped to the waist and with the breasts cut off. There was another woman with her head cut off and her body mutilated. There was a child with its stomach slashed open with a bayonet, and another—two or three years old—nailed to a door by its hands and feet. At Haecht 40 houses were burnt.

At *Thildonck* 31 houses were burnt and 10 civilians killed. Seven of those killed in the commune of Thildonck belonged to the family of the two Valckenaers brothers, whose farms (situated close to one another) were occupied by the Belgian troops early on the morn-

---

* d 125.
† 94.
‡ d 100-8.

ing of August 26th. As the Germans counter-attacked, the Belgian soldiers opened fire on them from the farm buildings and then retired. A platoon of Germans, with an officer at their head, entered Isodore Valckenaers' farm (where the whole family was gathered) about 8.o a.m. Isodore and two of his nephews—barely more than boys—were shot at once. His daughter, who clung to him and begged for his life, was torn away. The two young men were killed instantaneously. The elder, though horribly wounded by the bullet, survived, and was rescued next day. The rest of the family—a group of eleven women and children, for François-Edouard Valckenaers, the other brother, was away—were shot down half-an-hour later. They were herded together in the garden and fired on from all sides. Madame Isodore Valckenaers was holding her youngest baby in her arms. The bullet broke the child's arm and mangled its face, and then tore the mother's lip and destroyed one of her eyes. (The baby died, but the mother survived.) Madame F.-E. Valckenaers also survived—her dress was spattered with the brains of her fourteen-year-old son, whom she was holding by the hand. Five died altogether out of this group of eleven—some instantaneously, some after hours of agony. The eldest of them was only eighteen, the youngest was two-and-a-half. Thus seven of the Valckenaers' family were killed in all out of the fourteen present, and three were severely wounded. Only four were left unscathed.*

At *Werchter*† 267 houses were burnt and 162 sacked (out of 496), 15 civilians were killed, and 32 deported. The priests of *Wygmael* and *Wesemael* were dragged away as hostages, and driven, with a crowd of civilians from Herent, as a screen in front of the German troops on Aug. 29th. At Wesemael 46 houses were burnt, 13 civilians killed and 324 deported. At *Holsbeek* one civilian was killed and 35 houses burnt. In the whole *Canton of Haecht* 899 houses were burnt, 1,772 plundered, 116 civilians killed, and 647 deported.

As the Germans fell back south-eastward, the devastation spread into the Canton of Louvain. "When the Germans first arrived at *Herent*,"‡ states a witness (d 97), "they did nothing, but when they were repulsed from Malines they began to ill-treat the civilians." They shot a man at his door, and threw another man's body into a burning house. At *Aanbosch*, a hamlet of Herent, they dragged 4 men and 9 women out of their houses and bayonetted them. In the commune of Herent they killed 22 civilians (the priest was among the later victims)§ and deported 104 altogether, burned 312 houses and sacked 200. At

---

* R. pp. 378-380.
† d 110-1.
‡ d 95-9.
§ Mercier.

Velthem they killed 14 civilians and burned 44 houses. At *Winxele* they burned 57 houses and killed 5 civilians—the soldier who had shot and bayonetted one of them thrust his bayonet into the faces of the hostages: "Smell, smell! It is the blood of a Belgian pig" (d 97-8). At *Corbeek-Loo* 20 civilians were killed, 62 deported, and 129 houses burnt. At *Wilsele* 36 houses were burnt and 7 people killed. One of them was an epileptic who had a seizure while he was being carried away as a hostage. Since he could go no further, he was shot through the head (d 129). At *Kessel-Loo* 59 people were killed and 461 houses burnt; at *Linden* 6 and 103; at *Heverlé* 6 and 95. In the whole *Canton of Louvain* 2,441 houses were burnt, 2,722 plundered, 251 civilians killed, and 831 deported. About 40 per cent. of this destruction was done in the City of Louvain itself, on the night of August 25th and on the following nights and days. The destruction of Louvain was the greatest organised outrage which the Germans committed in the course of their invasion of Belgium and France, and as such it stands by itself. But it was also the inevitable climax of the outrages to which they had abandoned themselves in their retreat upon Louvain from Malines. The Germans burned and massacred invariably, wherever they passed, but there was a bloodthirstiness and obscenity in their conduct on this retreat which is hardly paralleled in their other exploits, and which put them in the temper for the supreme crime which followed.

(v) *Louvain.*

The Germans entered *Louvain* on August 19th. The Belgian troops did not attempt to hold the town, and the civil authorities had prepared for the Germans' arrival. They had called in all arms in private possession and deposited them in the Hôtel-de-Ville. This had been done a fortnight before the German occupation,* and was repeated, for security, on the morning of the 19th itself.† The municipal commissary of police remarked the exaggerated conscientiousness with which the order was obeyed. "Antiquarian pieces, flint-locks and even razors were handed in."‡ The people of Louvain were indeed terrified. They had heard what had happened in the villages round Liége, at Tongres and at St. Trond, and on the evening (August 18th) before the Germans arrived the refugees from Tirlemont had come pouring through the town.§ The Burgomaster, like his colleagues in other Belgian towns, had posted placards on August 18th, enjoining confidence and calm.

The German entry on the 19th took place without disturbance. Large requisitions were at once made on

* "Germans," p. 26.
† e23.
‡ R29; cp. "Germans," p. 9; Chambry, p. 14; e5; R24.
§ "Germans," p. 15; R24.

the town by the German Command. The troops were billeted on the inhabitants. In one house an officer demanded quarters for 50 men. "Revolver in hand, he inspected every bedroom minutely. 'If anything goes wrong, you are all *kaput*.' That was how he finished the business."* It was vacation time, and the lodgings of the University students were empty. Many houses were shut up altogether, and these were broken into and pillaged by the German soldiers.† They pillaged enormous quantities of wine, without interference on the part of their officers. "The soldiers did not scruple to drain in the street the contents of stolen bottles, and drunken soldiers were common objects."‡ There was also a great deal of wanton destruction— "furniture destroyed, mirrors and picture-frames smashed, carpets spoilt and so on."§ The house of Professor van Gehuchten, a scientist of international eminence, was treated with especial malice. This is testified by a number of people, including the Professor's son. "They destroyed, tore up and threw into the street my father's manuscripts and books (which were very numerous), and completely wrecked his library and its contents. They also destroyed the manuscript of an important work of my late father's which

---

* Chambry, p. 16..
† e2; R7, 10.
‡ R24; Chambry, p. 17.
§ "Horrors," p. 31.

was in the hands of the printer."*—"This misdemeanour made a scandal," states another witness. "It was brought to the knowledge of the German general, who seemed much put out, but took no measures of protection."† The pillage was even systematic. A servant, left by an absent professor in charge of his house, found on August 20th that the Germans "had five motor-vans outside the premises. I saw them removing from my master's house wine, blankets, books, etc., and placing them in the vans. They stripped the whole place of everything of value, including the furniture. . . . I saw them smashing glass and crockery and the windows."‡ On August 20th there were already acts of violence in the outskirts of the town. At Corbeek-Loo a girl of sixteen was violated by six soldiers and bayonetted in five places for offering resistance. Her parents were kept off with rifles.§ By noon on August 20th the town itself "was like a stable. Streets, pavements, public squares and trampled flower beds had disappeared under a layer of manure."‖

On August 20th the German military authorities covered the walls with proclamations: "Atrocities have been committed by (Belgian) franc-tireurs."¶—

* e25.
† R24; cp. R11; e2; "Germans," p. 25.
‡ e23.
§ e2; R18.
‖ "Germans," p. 25.
¶ "Germans," p. 26; R24.

"If anything happens to the German troops, *le total sera responsable*"* (an attempt to render in French the Prussian doctrine of collective responsibility). Doors must be left open at night. Windows fronting the street must be lighted up. Inhabitants must be within doors between 8.0 p.m. and 7.0 a.m. Most of these placards were ready-made in German, French and Russian. There were no placards in Flemish till after the events of August 25th. Yet Flemish was the only language spoken and understood by at least half the population of Louvain.

Hostages were also taken by the German authorities.† The Burgomaster, a City Councillor and a Senator were confined under guard in the Hôtel-de-Ville on the first day of occupation. From August 21st onwards they were replaced successively by other notables, including the Rector and Vice-Rector of the University. On August 21st there was another German proclamation, in which the inhabitants were called upon (for the third time) to deliver up their arms.‡ Requisitions and acts of pillage by individual officers and soldiers continued, and on the evening of August 24th the Burgomaster was dragged to the Railway Station and threatened with a revolver by a German officer, who had arrived with 250 men by train and demanded

* "Horrors," p. 31.
† R7, 24.
‡ R10.

17. MALINES: CARDINAL MERCIER'S STATE-ROOM AS A RED CROSS HOSPITAL

18. MALINES: THE CARDINAL'S THRONE-ROOM

a hot meal and mattresses for them at once. Major von Manteuffel, the Etappen-Kommandant in the city, was called in and the Burgomaster was released, but without reparation.* On that day, too, the German wounded were removed from Louvain†—an ominous precaution—and in the course of the following day there were spoken warnings.‡ On the morning of this day, Tuesday, August 25th, Madame Roomans, a notary's wife, is said to have been warned by the German officers billeted on her to leave the town. In the afternoon, about 5.0 o'clock, another lady reported how an officer, billeted on her and taking his leave, had added: "I hope you will be spared, for now it is going to begin." At supper time, when the first shots were fired and the alarm was sounded, officers billeted on various households are said to have exclaimed "Poor people!"—or to have wept.

On the morning of August 25th there were few German troops in Louvain. The greater part of those that had entered the town since the 19th had passed on to the front in the direction of Malines, and were now engaged in resisting the Belgian sortie from Antwerp, which was made this day. As the Belgian offensive made progress, the sound of the cannon became louder and louder in Louvain,§ and the German garrison grew

* R1, 24; "Germans," pp. 28-9.
† R29.
‡ R2, 24, 29.
§ "Germans," p. 31; Grondijs, p. 34; e 1; R1, 8, 11, 17.

increasingly uneasy. Despatch riders from the front
kept arriving at the Kommandantur;* at 4.0 o'clock
a general alarm was sounded;† the troops in the town
assembled and marched out towards the north-western
suburbs;‡ military waggons drove in from the north-
west in disorder, "their drivers grasping revolvers and
looking very much excited."§ At the same time, re-
inforcements‖ began to detrain at the *Station*, which
stands at the eastern extremity of the town, and is connected with the central *Grand' Place* and with the
University buildings by the broad, straight line of the
Rue de la Station, flanked with the private houses of
the wealthier inhabitants. These fresh troops were billeted hastily by their officers in the quarters nearest the
Station.¶ The cavalry were concentrated in the *Place
du Peuple*, a large square lying a short distance to the
left of the *Rue de la Station*, about half-way towards
the *Grand' Place*.** The square was already crowded
with the transport that had been sent back during the
day from the front.†† As the reinforcements kept on
detraining, and the quarters near the *Station* filled up,
the later arrivals went on to the *Grand' Place* and the

* "Germans," pp. 31-2.
† e 1.
‡ e 1; "Germans," p. 32; D7, 8.
§ "Germans," p. 32.
‖ "Germans," p. 32; Davignon, p. 97; R17.
¶ Chambry, p. 21; e3; R17.
** R7; D46.
†† D46.

Hôtel-de-Ville,* which was the seat of the Kommandantur.

During all this time the agitation increased. About 7.0 o'clock a company of Landsturm which had marched out in the afternoon to the north-western outskirts of the town, were ordered back by their battalion commander to the *Place de la Station*—the extensive square in front of the *station buildings*, out of which the *Rue de la Station* leads into the middle of the city.† The military police pickets‡ in the centre of the city were on the alert. Between 7.0 and 7.30 the alarm was sounded again,§ and the troops who had arrived that afternoon assembled from their billets and stood to arms.‖ The tension among them was extreme. They had been travelling hard all day; they had entered the town at dusk; it was now dark, and they did not know their way about the streets, nor from what quarter to expect the enemy forces, which were supposed to be on the point of making their appearance. It was in these circumstances that, a few minutes past eight o'clock, the shooting in Louvain broke out.

All parties agree that it broke out in answer to signals. A Belgian witness,¶ living near the *Tirlemont*

---

* D46.
† D7, 8.
‡ e1; R8.
§ R7, 17.
‖ Chambry, pp. 22-3.
¶ R6.

Gate, saw a German military motor-car dash up from the *Boulevard de Tirlemont*, make luminous signals at the Gate, and then dash off again. A fusillade immediately followed. The German troops bivouacked in the *Place de la Station* saw two rockets, the first green and the second red, rise in quick succession from the centre of the town.* They found themselves under fire immediately afterwards. A similar rocket was seen later in the night to rise above the conflagration.† It is natural to suppose that the rockets, as well as the lights on the car, were German military signals of the kind commonly used in European armies for signalling in the dark. There had been two false alarms already that afternoon and evening; there is nothing incredible in a third. The German troops in the *Place de la Station* assumed that the signals were of Belgian origin (and therefore of civilian origin, as the Belgian troops did not after all reach the town), because these signals were followed by firing directed against themselves. They could not believe that the shots were fired in error by their own comrades, yet there is convincing evidence that this was the case.

It is certain that German troops fired on each other in at least two places—in the *Rue de la Station* and in the *Rue de Bruxelles*, which leads into the *Grand' Place* from the opposite direction.

---

* D7, 10, 12, 13, 14-18, 22; cp. D46.
† R6.

19. Capelle-au-Bois

20, Capelle-au-Bois

"We were at supper," states a Belgian witness,* whose house was in the *Rue de la Station*, "when about 8.15, shots were suddenly fired in the street by German cavalry coming from the *Station*. The troops who were bivouacked in the square replied, and an automobile on its way to the *Station* had to stop abruptly opposite my house and reverse, while its occupants fired. Within a few seconds the din of revolver and rifle shots had become terrific. The fusillade was sustained, and spread (north-eastward) towards the *Boulevard de Diest*. It became so furious that there was even gun-fire. The encounter between the German troops continued as far as the *Grand' Place*, where on at least two occasions there was machine-gun fire. The fight lasted for from fifteen to twenty minutes with desperation; it persisted an hour longer after that, but with less violence."

"At the stroke of eight," states another witness,† "shots were heard by us, coming from the direction of the *Place du Peuple*, where the German cavalry was concentrated. Part of the baggage-train, which was stationed in the *Rue Léopold*, turned right about and went off at a gallop towards the *Station*. I was at my front door and heard the bullets whistling as they came from the *Place du Peuple*. At this moment a sustained

---

* R4.
† R7.

fusillade broke out, and there was a succession of cavalry-charges in the direction of the *Station*."

The stampede in the *Place du Peuple* is described by a German officer* who was present. "I heard the clock strike in a tower. . . . Complete darkness already prevailed. At the same moment I saw a green rocket go up above the houses south-west of the square. . . . Firing was directed on the German troops in the square. . . . Whilst riding round the square, I was shot from my horse on the north-eastern side. I distinctly heard the rattling of machine-guns, and the bullets flew in great numbers round about me. . . . After I had fallen from my horse, I was run over by an artillery transport waggon, the horses of which had been frightened by the firing and stampeded. . . ."

The shots by which this officer was wounded evidently came from German troops in the *Rue Léopold*, where they were attacking the house of Professor Verhelst. The Landsturm Company bivouacked in the *Station Square* was already replying vigorously to what it imagined to be the Belgian fire, coming from the *Rue Léopold* and the *Rue de la Station*.

"I stood with my Company," states the Company Commander,† "at about ten minutes to eight in the *Station Square*. I had stood about five minutes, when suddenly, quite unexpectedly, shots were fired at my

* D46.
† D8.

Company from the surrounding houses, from the windows, and from the attics. Simultaneously I heard lively firing from the *Rue de la Station*, as well as from all the neighbouring streets." (Precisely the district in which the newly-arrived troops had taken up their quarters.) "Shots were also fired from the windows of my hotel—straight from my room" (which had doubtless been occupied by some newly-arrived soldier during the afternoon, while the witness was on duty at the Malines Gate). . . .

"We now knelt down and fired at the opposite houses. . . . I sought cover with my Company in the entrances of some houses. During the assault five men of my Company were wounded. The fact that so few were wounded is due to the fact that the inhabitants were shooting too high. . . .

"About an hour later I was summoned to His Excellency General von Boehn, who was standing near by. His Excellency asked for an exact report, and, after I had made it, he said to me: 'Can you take an oath concerning what you have just reported to me— in particular, that the first shots were fired by the inhabitants from the houses?' I then answered: 'Yes, I can swear to that fact.'"

But what evidence had the Lieutenant for the "fact" to which he swore? There was no doubt about the shots, but he gives no proof of the identity of those who

99

fired them, and another witness,* who lived in a house looking on to the *Station Square*, is equally positive that the assailants, too, were German soldiers.

"Just before eight," he states, "we heard one shot from a rifle, followed immediately after by two others, and then a general fusillade began. I went at once to my garden; the bullets were passing quite close to me; I went back to the house and on to the balcony, and there I saw the Germans, not fighting Belgians, but fighting each other at a distance of 200 or 300 yards. At 8.0 o'clock it begins to be dark, but I am perfectly certain it was Germans fighting Germans. The firing on both sides passed right in front of my house, and from the other side of the railway. I was low down on the balcony, quite flat, and watched it all. They fought hard for about an hour. The officers whistled and shouted out orders; there was terrible confusion until each side found out they were fighting each other, and then the firing ceased. About half an hour after, on the other side of the railway, I heard a machine-gun—I was told afterwards that the Germans were killing civilians with it. It went on certainly for at least five or six minutes, stopping now and then for a few seconds. . . ."

This fighting near the *Station* seems to have been the first and fiercest of all, but the panic spread like wildfire through the city. It was spread by the horses

* e8.

that stampeded in the *Place du Peuple* and elsewhere, and galloped riderless in all directions—across the *Station Square*,* through the suburb of *Corbeek-Loo*,† down the *Rue de la Station*,‡ and up the *Rue de Tirle-mont*,§ the *Rue de Bruxelles*,‖ and the *Rue de Ma-lines*.¶ The troops infected by the panic either ran amok or took to flight.

"About 8.0 o'clock," states a witness,** "the *Rue de la Station* was the scene of a stampede of horses and baggage waggons, some of which were overturned. A smart burst of rifle-fire occurred at this moment. This came from the German police-guard in the *Rue de la Station*, who, seeing troops arrive in disorder, thought that it was the enemy. Another proof of their mistake is that later during the same night a group of German soldiers, under the command of an officer, got into a shop belonging to the F.'s and in charge of their nephew B., and told him, pointing their revolvers at him, to hide them in the cellar. A few hours after-wards, hearing troops passing, they compelled him to go and see if it was the French or the Germans, and when they learnt that it was the Germans, they called

---

* D8, 22.
† R20.
‡ R3.
§ "Germans," p. 33.
‖ R3.
¶ R13.
** e 1; cp. R2

out: 'Then we are safe,' and rejoined their compatriots."

These new troops hurrying into the town in the midst of the uproar were infected by the panic in their turn and flung themselves into the fighting. "On August 25th," states one of them in his diary,* "we hold ourselves on the alert at *Grimde* (a sugar refinery); here, too, everything is burnt and destroyed. From *Grimde* we continue our march upon Louvain; here it is a picture of horror all round; corpses of our men and horses; motor-cars blazing; the water poisoned; we have scarcely reached the outskirts of the town when the fusillade begins again more merrily than ever; naturally we wheel about and sweep the street; then the town is peppered by us thoroughly."

In the *Rue Léopold*, leading from the *Rue de la Station* into the *Place du Peuple*, "at 8.0 o'clock exactly a violent fusillade broke out." The newly-arrived troops, who had been under arms since the alarm at 7.0 o'clock, "took to flight as fast as their legs could carry them. From our cellar," states one of the householders on whom they had been billeted,† "we saw them running until they must have been out of breath."

There was a single shot, followed by a fusillade and machine-gun fire, in the *Rue des Joyeuses Entrées*.‡

* Morgan, p. 102.
† Chambry, p. 23.
‡ R2.

Waggons and motor-cars were flying out of the town down the *Rue de Parc*, and soldiers on foot down the *Rue de Tirlemont*.* In the *Rue des Flamands*, which runs at right-angles between these two latter roads, "at ten minutes past eight, a shot was fired quite close to the *Institut Supérieur de Philosophie*" (now converted into the *Hôpital St. Thomas*). "We had scarcely taken note of it," states one of the workers in the hospital,† "when other reports followed. In less than a minute rifle-shots and machine-gun fire mingled in a terrific din. Accompanying the crack of the firearms, we heard the dull thud of galloping hoofs in the *Rue de Tirlemont*."

Mgr. Deploige, President of the Institute and Director of the Hospital, reports‡ that "a lively fusillade broke out suddenly at 8.0 o'clock (Belgian time), at different points simultaneously—at the *Brussels Gate*, at the *Tirlemont Gate*, in the *Rue de la Station*, *Rue Léopold*, *Rue Marie-Thérèse*, *Rue des Joyeuses Entrées*, *Rue de Tirlemont*, etc.§ It was the German troops firing with rifles and machine-guns. Some houses were literally riddled with bullets, and a number of civilians were killed in their homes."

Higher up the *Rue de Tirlemont*, in the direction of

---

* "Horrors," p. 38.
† "Germans," p. 33.
‡ R27.
§ Also in the *Rue Vital Decoster*, north of the *Rue de la Station* (R13).

the *Grand' Place*, there was a Belgian Infantry Barracks, which had been turned into a hospital for slightly
incapacitated German soldiers. The patients were in
a state of nervous excitement already. "Every man,"
states one of them,* "had his rifle by his side, also
ball-cartridge."—"About 9.0 o'clock," states another,†
"we heard shots . . . We had to fall in in the yard.
A sergeant-major distributed cartridges among us,
whereupon I marched out with about 20 men. In the
Rue de Tirlemont a lively fire was directed against us
from guns of small bore. . . . We pushed our way into
a restaurant from which shots had come, and found in
the proprietor's possession about 100 Browning cartridges. He was arrested and shot."—"We now," continues the former, "stormed all the houses out of which
shots were being fired. . . . Those who were found
with weapons were immediately shot or bayonetted.
. . . I myself, together with a comrade, bayonetted
one inhabitant who went for me with his knife. . . ."

But who would not defend himself with a knife when
attacked by an armed man breaking into his house?
The witness admits that only five civilians were armed
out of the twenty-five dragged out. Were these
"armed" with knives? Or if revolver bullets were
found in their houses, was it proved that they had not
delivered up their revolvers at the time when they had

---

* D29; cp. R2.
† D20; cp. D25, 27.

been ordered to do so by the municipal authorities and the German Command? The witness does not claim to have found the revolvers themselves as well as the ammunition, though even if he had that was no proof that his victims had been firing with them, or even that they were theirs. The German Army uses "Brownings" too, and at this stage of the panic many German soldiers had broken into private houses and were firing from the windows as points of vantage. Two German soldiers broke into the house of Professor Verhelst (*Rue Léopold, 16*), and fired into the street out of the second storey window. Other Germans passing shouted: "They have been shooting here," and returned the fire.* Mgr. Ladeuze, Rector of Louvain University, was looking from the window of his house adjoining the garden of the *Chemical Institute, Rue de Namur,* and saw two German soldiers hidden among the trees and firing over the wall into the street.† Moreover, there is definite evidence of Germans firing on one another by mistake in other quarters beside the neighbourhood of the *Station.*

"I myself know," declares a Belgian witness,‡ "that the Germans fired on one another on August 25th. On that day, at about 8.0 p.m., I was in the *Rue de Bruxelles* at Louvain. I was hidden in a house. There

* "Germans," pp. 41, 107; e24; R29.
† "Germans," p. 107; Grondijs p. 58.
‡ e5; cp. e13; R10.

was one party of German soldiers at one end of the street firing on another party at the other end. I could see that this happened myself. On the next day I spoke to a German soldier called Hermann Otto—he was a private in a Bavarian regiment. He told me that he himself was in the *Rue de Bruxelles* the evening before, and that the two parties firing on one another were Bavarians and Poles, he being among the Bavarians. . . ."

The Poles openly blamed the Bavarians for the error. A wounded Polish Catholic, who was brought in during the night to the Dominican Monastery in the *Rue Juste-Lipse*, told the monks that "he had been wounded by a German bullet in an exchange of shots between two groups of German soldiers."* On the Thursday following, a wounded Polish soldier was lying in the hospital of the Sisters of Mary at Wesemael, and, seeing German troops patrolling the road between Wesemael and Louvain, exclaimed to one of the nuns: "These drunken pigs fired on us."†

The casualties inflicted by the Germans on each other do not, however, appear to have been heavy. One German witness‡ saw "two dead transport horses and several dead soldiers" lying in the *Place du Peuple*. Another§ saw a soldier lying near the *Juste-Lipse*

* xxi p. 115.
† R5.
‡ D20.
§ D9.

Monument who had been killed by a shot through the mouth. But most express astonishment at the lightness of the losses caused by so heavy a fire. "It is really a miracle," said a German military doctor to a Belgian Professor in the course of the night,* "that not one soldier has been wounded by this violent fusillade." —"A murderous fire," states the surgeon of the Second Neuss Landsturm Battalion,† "was directed against us from *Rue de la Station, No. 120.* The fact that we or some of us were not killed I can merely explain by the fact that we were going along the same side of the street from which the shots were fired, and that it was night."—"A tremendous fire," states Major von Manteuffel, the Etappen-Kommandant,‡ "was opened from the houses surrounding the *Grand' Place,* which was now filled with artillery (one battery), and with transport columns, motor-lorries and tanks of benzine. . . . I believe there were three men wounded, chiefly in the legs." General von Boehn, commanding the Ninth Reserve Army Corps, estimates§ that the total loss, in killed, wounded, and missing, of his General Command Staff, which was stationed in the *Place du Peuple,* "amounts to 5 officers, 2 officials, 23 men, and 95 horses."—"I note that the inhabitants fired far too

* R13.
† D9.
‡ D3.
§ D1.

high," states a N.C.O. of the Landsturm Company drawn up in the *Station Square*.* "That was our good luck, because otherwise, considering the fearful fire which was directed against us from all the houses in the *Station Square*, most German officers and soldiers would have been killed or seriously wounded."

Thus the German troops in Louvain seem not merely to have fired on one another, but to have exaggerated hysterically the amount of danger each incurred from the other's mistake. And the legend grew with time. The deposition last quoted was taken down on September 17th, 1914, less than a month after the event. But when examined again, on November 19th, the same witness deposed that "Many of us were wounded, and some of us even received mortal wounds. . . . I fully maintain my evidence of September 17th," he naïvely adds in conclusion.

On the night of August 25th these German soldiers were distraught beyond all restraints of reason and justice. They blindly assumed that it was the civilians, and not their comrades, who had fired, and when they discovered their error they accused the civilians, deliberately, to save their own reputation.

The Director and the Chief Surgeon of the *Hôpital St.-Thomas* went out into the street after the first fusillade was over. Three soldiers with fixed bayonets rushed at them shouting: "You fired! Die!"—and it

---

* D10.

was only with difficulty that they persuaded them to spare their lives. When the firing began again a sergeant broke into the hospital shouting: "Who fired here?"—and placed the hospital staff under guard.* This was the effect of panic, but there were cases in which the firing was imputed to civilians, and punishment meted out for it, by means of criminal trickery. It was realised that the material evidence would be damning to the German Army. The empty cartridge cases were all German which were picked up in the streets,† and it is stated that every bullet extracted from the bodies of wounded German soldiers was found to be of German origin.‡ The Germans, convicted by these proofs, shrank from no fraud which might enable them to transfer the guilt on to the heads of Belgian victims.

"The Germans took the horses out of a Belgian Red Cross car," states a Belgian witness§ living in the *Station Square*, "frightened them so that they ran down the street, and then shot three of them. Two fell quite close to my house. They then took a Belgian artillery helmet and put it on the ground, so as to prepare a *mise-en-scène* to pretend that the Belgians had been fighting in the street."

---

* "Germans" pp. 33-5.
† R25.
‡ R29 (Statement by the Abbé van den Bergh, accredited by His Eminence Cardinal Piffl, Prince-Bishop of Vienna, to conduct inquiries on behalf of the Wiener Priester-Verein); cp. R25.
§ e8.

At a late hour of the night a detachment of German soldiers was passing one of the professors' houses, when a shot rang out, followed by a volley from the soldiers through the windows of the house. The soldiers then broke in and accused the inmates of having fired the first shot. They were mad with fury, and the professor and his family barely escaped with their lives. A sergeant pointed to his boot, with the implication that the shot had struck him there; but a witness in another house actually saw this sergeant fire the original shot himself, and make the same gesture after it to incite his comrades.*

A staff-surgeon billeted on a curé in the suburb of *Blauwput* pretended he had been wounded by civilians when he had really fallen from a wall. On the morning of the 26th the officer in local command arrested fifty-seven men at *Blauwput*, this curé included, in order to decimate them in reprisal for wounds which the surgeon and two other soldiers had received. The curé was exempted by the lot, when the surgeon came up with a handful of revolver-cartridges which he professed to have discovered in the curé's house. The officer answered: "Go away. I have searched this house myself," and the surgeon slunk off. The curé was not added to the victims, but every tenth man was shot all the same.†

---

* R3; cp. e24.
† R29; cp. e26.

That "the civilians had fired" was already an official dogma with the German military authorities in Louvain. Mgr. Coenraets, Vice-Rector of the University, was serving that day as a hostage at the *Hôtel-de-Ville*. A Dominican monk, Father Parijs, was there at the moment the firing broke out, in quest of a pass for remaining out-of-doors at night on ambulance service. He was now retained as well, and Alderman Schmit was fetched from his house. Von Boehn, the General Commanding the Ninth Reserve Corps, harangued these hostages on his arrival from the Malines front, and von Manteuffel, the Etappen-Kommandant, then conducted them, with a guard of soldiers, round the town. Baron Orban de Xivry was dragged out of his house to join them on the way. The procession halted at intervals in the streets, and the four hostages were compelled to proclaim to their fellow-citizens, in Flemish and in French, that, unless the firing ceased, the hostages themselves would be shot, the town would have to pay an indemnity of 20,000,000 francs, the houses from which shots were fired would be burnt, and artillery-fire would be directed upon Louvain as a whole.*

But "reprisals" against the civil population had already begun. The firing from German soldiers in the houses upon German soldiers in the street was answered by a general assault of the latter upon all houses within

---

*Dr (von Boehn), 2, 3 (von Manteuffel), 9, 49 (2).

their reach. "They broke the house-doors," states a Belgian woman,* "with the butt-ends of their rifles. . . . They shot through the gratings of the cellars."— "In the *Hôtel-de-Ville*," states von Manteuffel,† "I saw the Company stationed there on the ground floor, standing at the windows and answering the fire of the inhabitants. In front of the *Hôtel-de-Ville*, on the entrance steps, I also saw soldiers firing in reply to the inhabitants' fire in the direction of their houses."— "Personally I was under the distinct impression," states a staff officer,‡ "that we were fired at from the Hôtel Maria Theresa with machine-guns." (This is quite probable, and merely proves that those who fired were German soldiers.) "The fire from machine-guns lasted from four to five minutes, and was immediately answered by our troops, who finally stormed the house and set it on fire."—"The order was passed up from the rear that we should fire into the houses," states an infantryman who had just detrained and was marching with his unit into the town.§ "Thereupon we shot into the house-fronts on either side of us. To what extent the fire was answered I cannot say, the noise and confusion were too great."—"We now dispersed towards both sides," states a lance-corporal in the same

---

* e13; cp. R17, 24.
† D3.
‡ D2; cp. D11.
§ D36 (1).

21. CAPELLE-AU-BOIS: THE CHURCH

22. LOUVAIN: NEAR THE CHURCH OF ST. PIERRE

battalion,* "and fired into the upper windows. . . . How long the firing lasted I cannot say. . . . We now began shooting into the ground-floor windows too, as well as tearing down a certain number of the shutters. I made my way into the house from which the shot had come, with a few others who had forced open the door. We could find no one in the house. In the room from which the shot had come there was, however, a petroleum lamp, lying overturned on the table and still smouldering. . . ."

These assaults on houses passed over inevitably into wholesale incendiarism. "The German troops," as the Editors of the German White Book remark in their summarising report on the events at Louvain, "had to resort to energetic counter-measures. In accordance with the threats, the inhabitants who had taken part in the attack were shot, and the houses from which shots had been fired were set on fire. The spreading of the fire to other houses also and the destruction of some streets could not be avoided. In this way the Cathedral" (*i. e.*, the Collegiate Church of St. Pierre) "also caught fire. . . ."

There is a map in the German White Book which shows the quarters burnt down. The incendiarism started in the *Station Square*, and spread along the *Boulevard de Tirlemont* as far as the *Tirlemont Gate*. It was renewed across the railway and devastated the

---

* D36 (2).

suburbs to the east. Then it was extended up the *Rue de la Station* into the heart of the town, and here the *Church of St. Pierre* was destroyed, and the *University Halles* with the priceless *University Library*—not by mischance, as the German Report alleges, but by the deliberate work of German troops, employing the same incendiary apparatus as had been used already at Visé, Liége and elsewhere.*

The burning was directed by a German officer from the *Vieux Marché*, a large open space near the centre of the town, and by another group of officers stationed in the *Place du Peuple.†* The burning here is described by a German officer‡ (whose evidence on other points has been quoted above). "The Company," he states, "continued to fire into the houses. The fire of the inhabitants (*sic*) gradually died down. Thereupon the German soldiers broke in the doors of the houses and set the houses on fire, flinging burning petroleum lamps into the houses or striking off the gas-taps, setting light to the gas which rushed out and throwing table-cloths and curtains into the flames. Here and there benzine was also employed as a means of ignition. The order to set fire to the houses was given out

---

* *Area of incendiarism:* "Eye-witness" p. 1; "Horrors" pp. 39, 43; "Germans" pp. 35-8, 92; Chambry pp. 25, 92; *Apparatus:* e2, 13; R8, 13; cp. also D31, 37 (2).

† R24.

‡ D46.

by Colonel von Stubenrauch, whose voice I distinguished. . . ."

In the *Rue de la Station* the Germans set the houses on fire with incendiary bombs. This was seen by a Belgian witness,* and is confirmed by the German officer just cited, who, in the *Place du Peuple*, "heard repeatedly the detonation of what appeared to be heavy guns" round about him. "I supposed," he proceeds, "that artillery was firing; but since there was none present, there is only one explanation for this—that the inhabitants (*sic*) also threw hand-grenades."

In the *Rue de Manège*† another Belgian witness saw a soldier pouring inflammable liquid over a house from a bucket, and this though a German military surgeon, present on the spot, admitted that in that house there had been nobody firing. Soldiers are also stated to have been seen‡ with a complete incendiary equipment (syringe, hatchet, etc.), and with "Gott mit Uns" and "Company of Incendiaries" blazoned on their belts. The Germans deny that the *Church of St. Pierre* was deliberately burnt, and allege that the fire spread to it from private houses;§ but a Dutch witness‖ saw it burning while the adjoining houses were still intact. There is less evidence for the deliberate burning of the

---

* R8; e23; cp. "Germans" p. 46.
† R13; cp. e14, 28.
‡ e13; cp. e24.
§ D4.
‖ R14 (Grondijs); cp. R19, 29.

University Halles, containing the *Library*, but it is significant that the building was completely consumed in one night (a result hardly possible without artificial means), and at 11.0 p.m., in the middle of the burning, an officer answered a Belgian monk, who protested, that it was "By Order."* The manuscripts and early printed books in the *Library* were one of the treasures of Europe. The whole collection of 250,000 volumes was the intellectual capital of the University, without which it could not carry on its work. Every volume and manuscript was destroyed. The Germans pride themselves on saving the *Hôtel-de-Ville*, but they saved it because it was the seat of the German Kommandantur, and this only suggests that, had they desired, they could have prevented the destruction of the other buildings as well.

As the houses took fire the inhabitants met their fate. Some were asphyxiated in the cellars where they had taken refuge from the shooting, or were burnt alive as they attempted to escape from their homes.† Others were shot down by the German troops as they ran out into the street,‡ or while they were fighting the flames.§ "The franc-tireurs," as they are called by the German officer in the *Place du Peuple*,‖ "were without excep-

---

* R29; cp. "Eye-witness" p. 3; "Germans" p. 37; R25.
† e2, 23; R10, 11, 18, 24.
‡ e1; R8.
§ R10.
‖ D46.

23. LOUVAIN: THE CHURCH OF ST. PIERRE

24. Louvain: The Church of St. Pierre Across the Ruins

tion evil-looking figures, such as I have never seen elsewhere in all my life. They were shot down by the
German posts stationed below. . . ."

Others, again, tried to save themselves by climbing
garden walls.* "I, my mother and my servants,"
states one of these,† "took refuge at A.'s, whose cellars are vaulted and therefore afforded us a better protection than mine. A little later we withdrew to A.'s
stables, where about 30 people, who had got there by
climbing the garden walls, were to be found. Some of
these poor wretches had had to climb 20 walls. A
ring came at the bell. We opened the door. Several
civilians flung themselves under the porch. The Germans were firing upon them from the street."

"When we were crossing a particularly high wall,"
states another victim,‡ "my wife was on the top of
the wall and I was helping her to get down, when a
party of 15 Germans came up with rifles and revolvers.
They told us to come down. My wife did not follow
as quickly as they wished. One of them made a lunge
at her with his bayonet. I seized the blade of the
bayonet and stopped the lunge. The German soldier
then tried to stab me in the face with his bayonet. . . .

"They kept hitting us with the butt-ends of their
rifles—the women and children as well as the men.

---

* R8, 26; e14.
† e1.
‡ e8; cp. "Horrors" p. 39; e17; R8, 15, 17.

They struck us on the elbows because they said our arms were not raised high enough. . . .

"We were driven in this way through a burning house to the *Place de la Station*. There were a number of prisoners already there. In front of the station entrance there were the corpses of three civilians killed by rifle fire. The women and the children were separated. The women were put on one side and the men on the other. One of the German soldiers pushed my wife with the butt-end of his rifle, so that she was compelled to walk on the three corpses. Her shoes were full of blood. . . .

"Other prisoners were being continually brought in. I saw one prisoner with a bayonet-wound behind his ear. A boy of fifteen had a bayonet-wound in his throat in front. . . . The priests were treated more brutally than the rest. I saw one belaboured with the butt-ends of rifles. Some German soldiers came up to me sniggering, and said that all the women were going to be raped. . . . They explained themselves by gestures. . . . The streets were full of empty wine bottles. . . .

"An officer told me that he was merely executing orders, and that he himself would be shot if he did not execute them. . . ."

The battue of civilians through the streets was the final horror of that night. The massacre began with the murder of M. David-Fischbach. He was a man of property, a benefactor of the University and the town. Since the outbreak of war he had given 10,000 francs to the Red Cross. Since the German occupation he had entertained German officers in his house, which stood in the *Rue de la Station* opposite the *Statue of Juste-Lipse*, and about 9.0 o'clock that evening he had gone to bed.

"Close to the *Monument Square*," states Dr. Berg- hausen, the German military surgeon who was responsible for M. David-Fischbach's death,* "I saw a German soldier lying dead on the ground. . . . His comrades told me that the shot had been fired from the corner house belonging to David-Fischbach. Thereupon I myself, with my servant, broke in the door of the house and met first the owner of the house, old David-Fischbach. I challenged him concerning the soldier who had been murdered. . . . Old David-Fischbach declared he knew nothing about it. Thereupon his son, young Fischbach, came downstairs from the first floor, and from the porter's lodge appeared an old servant. I immediately took father, son, and servant with me into the street. At that moment a tumult arose in the street, because a fearful fusillade had opened from a few houses on the same side of the street against the soldiers standing by the Monument and against myself. In the darkness I then lost sight of David-Fischbach, with his son and servant. . . ."

---

* D9; cp. R24; e14 (M. David-Fischbach's servant).

The soldiers set the old man with his back against the statue. Standing with his arms raised, he had to watch his house set on fire. Then he was bayonetted and finally shot to death. His son was shot, too. His house was burnt to the ground, and a servant asphyxiated in the cellar.*

"Later," adds Dr. Berghausen, "I met Major von Manteuffel with the hostages, and all four or five of us saw the dead soldier lying in front of the monument and, a few steps further on, old David-Fischbach. I assumed that the comrades of the soldier who had been killed . . . had at once inflicted punishment on, the owner of the house. . . ."

The corpse was also seen by a professor's wife who made her way to the *Hôpital St.-Thomas*—the old man's white beard was stained with blood.†

The massacre spread. Six workmen returning from their work were shot down from behind.‡ A woman was shot as she was beating for admittance on a door.§ A man had his hands tied behind his back, and was shot as he ran down the street.‖ Another witness saw 20 men shot.¶ One saw 19 corpses,** and corpses were also seen with their hands tied behind their backs,

---

* Chambry pp. 26-7.
† "Germans" p. 42.
‡ e16.
§ e1.
‖ e15.
¶ e17.
** e15.

like the victim mentioned above.* There was the body of a woman cut in two, with a child still alive beside her.† Other children had been murdered, and were lying dead.‡ There was the body of another murdered woman, and a girl of fourteen who had been wounded and was being carried to hospital. A German soldier beckoned a Dutch witness into a shop,§ and showed him the shop-keeper's body in the backroom, in a night-shirt, with a bullet-wound through the head.

These were the "evil-looking franc-tireurs" whom the German soldiers shot down at sight. Inhabitants of Louvain dragged as prisoners through the streets‖ recognised the corpses of people they knew. Here a bootmaker lay,¶ here a hairdresser,¶ here a professor. The corpse of Professor Lenertz was lying in front of his house in the *Boulevard de Tirlemont*. It was recognised by Dr. Noyons, one of his colleagues (though a Dutchman by nationality), who was serving in the *Hôpital St.-Thomas*, and so escaped himself.** "On the 27th," states a Belgian lady,†† "M. Lenertz' body was still

---

* e19.
† e17.
‡ e13.
§ Grondijs p. 39.
‖ "Germans" pp. 46-7.
¶ R19.
** "Germans" p. 43.
†† R2.

lying on the Boulevard. When his wife and children were evicted by the Germans and came out of their house, members of the family had to stand in front of the body to hide it from Madame Lenertz' sight."

The dead were lying in every quarter of the town. In the *Boulevard de Tirlemont* there were six or seven more.* There was one at the end of the *Rue du Manège*.† But the greatest number were in the *Station Square*, where they were seen by all the civilian prisoners herded thither this night and the following day.‡ Their murder is described by a German sergeant-major§ who was fighting in the neighbourhood of the *Station*. "Various civilians," he remarks, "were led off by my men, and after judgment had been given against them by the Commandant, they were shot in the *Square* in front of the *Station*. In accordance with orders, I myself helped to set fire to various houses, after having in every case previously convinced myself that no one was left in them. Towards midnight the work was done, and the Company returned to the station buildings, before which were lying shot about 15 inhabitants of the town."

The slaughter itself increased the thirst for blood. A Dutch witness‖ met a German column marching in

---

* R11, 17.
† R13.
‡ e1, 9, 13; R7, 8, 26.
§ D37 (2).
‖ Grondijs p. 41.

from *Aerschot*. "The soldiers were beside themselves with rage at the sight of the corpses, and cried: 'Schweinhunde! Schweinhunde!' They regarded me with threatening eyes. I passed on my way. . . ."

The soldiers in their frenzy respected no one. The Hostel for Spanish students in the *Rue de la Station* was burnt down, though it was protected by the Spanish flag. Father Catala, the Superior of the Hostel and formerly Vice-Consul of Spain, barely escaped with his life. There was no mercy either for the old or the sick. A retired barrister, bedridden with paralysis, had his house burnt over his head, and was brought to the *Hôpital St.-Thomas* to die. Another old man, more than eighty years old and in his last illness, was cast out by the soldiers into the street, and died in the *Hôpital St.-Thomas* next day.* An aged concierge was cast alive into the blazing ruins of the house it was his duty to guard.† So it went on till dawn, when the havoc was completed by salvoes of artillery. "At four o'clock in the morning," states an officer of the Ninth German Reserve Corps Staff,‡ "the Army Corps moved out to battle. We did not enter the main streets, but advanced along an avenue. . . . As the road carrying our lines of communication was continuously fired on, the order was given to clear the town by

* "Germans" pp. 43-5; c2.
† R24.
‡ D2.

force. Two guns were sent with 150 shells. The two guns, firing from the *Railway Station*, swept the streets with shells. Thus at least the quarter surrounding the *Railway Station* was secured, and this made it possible to conduct the supply-columns through the town. . . ."

It was now the morning of August 26th. At dawn Mgr. Coenraets and Father Parijs, the hostages of the preceding night, were placed under escort and marched round the City once more. If the firing continued the hostages were to be shot. They had to proclaim this themselves to the inhabitants from point to point of the town, and they were kept at this task till far on in the day.* The inhabitants, meanwhile, were paying the penalty for the shots which not they but the Germans had already fired.

In one street after another the people were dragged from their houses, and those not slaughtered out of hand were driven by the soldiers to the *Station Square*. "I only had slippers on," states one victim,† "and no hat or waistcoat. On the way to the *Station Square*, soldiers kicked me and hit me with the butt-ends of their rifles, and shouted: 'Oh, you swine! Another who shot at us! You swine!' My hands were tied behind my back with a cord, and when I cried: 'Oh, God, you are hurting me,' a soldier spat on me."—— "We had to go in front of the soldiers," adds this

---

* "Horrors" p. 40; "Germans" p. 47; xxi p. 115; R6, 10.
† e3.

25. Louvain: The Church of St. Pierre—Interior.

26. LOUVAIN: STATION SQUARE

witness's wife,* "holding our hands above our heads. All the ladies who lived in the Boulevard—invalids or not—were taken prisoners. One of them, an old lady of 85, who could scarcely walk, was dragged from her cellar with her maid."

When they reached the *Station Square* the men were herded to one side, the women and children to the other. It was done by an officer with a loaded revolver.† "We were separated from our families," states one of the men;‡ "we were knocked about and blows were rained on us from rifle butts; the women and children and the men were isolated from one another. . . ."

The men's pockets were rifled. Purses, keys, penknives and so on were taken from them.§ One gentleman's servant had 7,805 francs taken from his bag, and was given a receipt for 7,000 francs in exchange.|| This was the preliminary to a "trial," conducted by Captain Albrecht,¶ a staff officer of the Ninth Reserve Corps. "The soldiers," states a German tradesman who acted as Captain Albrecht's interpreter,** "brought forward the civilians whom they had seized, . . . In all about 600 persons may have been brought

* e4; cp. R7.
† e1 = R8; cp. R1, 7.
‡ R17.
§ e3.
|| e1 = R8.
¶ Killed, October, 1914.
** D38.

in, the lives of at least 500 of whom were spared, because no clear proof of their guilt seemed to be established at the trial. These persons were set on one side. . . . Captain Albrecht followed the course—I imagine, by the command of his superiors—of ordering that those among the men brought forward upon whom either a weapon or an identification mark was discovered, or in whose case it was established by at least two witnesses that they had fired upon the German troops, should be shot. It is an utter impossibility, according to my firm conviction, that any innocent man should have lost his life. . . ."

But was there really "clear proof of guilt" in any of these cases? Not one of these "identification marks" (assumed to establish that the bearer was a member of the Belgian Army) has been brought forward as material evidence by the German Government. And was the other material evidence so clear? One man, for instance,* had a German bullet in his pocket which he had picked up in the street. "He was shot down, and two of his comrades had to make a pit and bury him in the place where he was shot."† One priest was shot "because he had purposely enticed the soldiers, according to their testimony, under the fire of the franc-tireurs."‡ Two other priests were shot "for distribut-

* e4; cp. R20.
† e4.
‡ D38.

ing ammunition to civilians,"* but this was only a story heard from General Headquarters at second-hand. The witness who tells it was sent with a squad "to set on fire two hotels in the *Station Square* and drive out their inmates. The chief culprits found, apparently, a way of escape in good time over the roofs, since only the proprietor of one of the hotels presented himself at 5.0 o'clock in the morning, and very shortly afterwards received the reward he deserved." But what was the proof that he deserved it? Not any material evidence on his person, or the testimony of two witnesses who had seen him fire, but simply the fact that he was the only Belgian found in a certain building the inmates of which had been condemned, *a priori*, as franc-tireurs. The logic of this proceeding is defended by the tradesman interpreter, who submits† that "apart from all evidence, the persons brought to trial must have acted somehow in a suspicious manner —otherwise they would never have been brought to trial at all."

"It is untrue," nevertheless he states expressly, "that an arbitrary selection among the persons brought forward was made when the order for execution was issued." But one of the Belgian women‡ held prisoner in the *Station Square* describes how "the men were

---

* D48.
† D38.
‡ e13.

placed in rows of five, and the fifth in each row was taken and shot," as she affirms, "in my presence. If the fifth man happened to be old, his place was taken by the sixth man if he happened to be younger. This was also witnessed by my grandmother, my uncle and his wife, my cousin and our servant. . . ."

"The whole day long," states another Belgian woman,* "I saw civilians being shot—twenty to twenty-five of them, including some monks or priests— in the *Station Square* and the *Boulevard de Tirlemont*, opposite the warehouse. The victims were bound four together and placed on the pavement in front of the Maison Hamaide. The soldiers who shot them were on the other side of the Boulevard, on the warehouse roof. For that matter, the soldiers were firing everywhere in all directions."

The executions were also witnessed by the German troops. "On the morning of August 26th," states a soldier,† "I saw many civilians, more than a hundred, among them five priests, shot at the *Station Square* in Louvain because they had fired on German troops or because weapons were found on their persons."

This went on all day, and all day the women were compelled to watch it, while the surviving men were marched away in batches, and the houses on either side of the railway continued to burn. When night came

* R9.
† D19; cp. D37 (3), 41, 43.

the women were confined in the *Station*. "My aunt,"
continues the witness quoted above,* "was taken to
the *Station* with her baby and kept there till the morning. It rained all the night, and she wrapped the baby
in her skirt. The baby cried for food, and a German
soldier gave the child a little water, and took my aunt
and the child to an empty railway-carriage. Some
other women got into the carriage with her, but during
the whole night the Germans fired at the carriage for
amusement. . . ."

The firing by German soldiers had never ceased since
the first outbreak at 8.0 o'clock the evening before. An
eye-witness records two bursts of it on the 26th—one
at 5.0 p.m., and a more serious one at 8.45.† This
firing was due in part to panic, but was in part of a
more deliberate character. "The whole day," states a
Belgian witness,‡ "the soldiers went and came through
the streets, saying: 'Man hat geschossen,' but it seems
that the shots came from the soldiers themselves. I
myself saw a soldier going through the streets shooting
peacefully in the air." There was also killing in cold
blood. A café proprietor and his daughter were shot
by two German soldiers waiting to be served. The
other daughter crept under a table and escaped.§

---

* e13; cp. Chambry pp. 38-9.
† "Eye-witness" p. 4; cp. "Horrors" p. 39; Chambry pp. 33, 71-2;
D37 (2).
‡ e2.
§ Grondijs pp. 50-1.

The women held prisoner at the *Station* were only
released at 8.0 o'clock on the morning of the 27th,*
but they had suffered less during these hours than the
men. "Of the men," as a German witness puts it,†
"some were shot according to Martial Law. In the
case of a large number of others it was, however, impossible to determine whether they had taken part in
the shooting. These persons were placed for the moment in the *Station;* some of them were conveyed
elsewhere."

The first batch‡ of those "not found guilty" was
"conveyed" by the *Boulevard de Diest* round the outskirts of the town, and out along the *Malines Road*,
about 11.0 o'clock in the morning. It consisted of
from 70 to 80 men, one of whom at least was 75 years
old, while five were neutrals—a Paraguayan priest,
Father Gamarra,§ the Superior of the Spanish Hostel,
Father Catala, and three of Father Catala's students.
There were doctors, lawyers, and retired officers among
the Belgian victims. One prisoner was driven on
ahead to warn the country people that all the hostages
would be executed if a single shot were fired;‖ the
rest were searched, had their hands bound behind their
backs, and were marched in column under guard. On

* e4; R9.
† D44.
‡ R1, 7, 8 (=e1), 20, 26.
§ R26 (his deposition) ; cp. Grondijs, pp. 70-1.
‖ R1, 8 (=e1).

the way to *Herent* they were used as a screen.* The
village of *Herent* was burning, and they had to run
through the street to avoid being scorched by the
flames.† "Carbonised corpses were lying in front of
the houses."—"At *Herent*," states the South American
priest,‡ "I saw lying in the nook of a wall the corpse
of a girl twelve or thirteen years old, who had been
burnt alive." On the road from *Herent* to *Bueken*
"everything was ·devastated." Beyond *Bueken* and
Campenhout they were made to halt in a field, and
were told that they were going to be executed. Squads
of soldiers advanced on them from the front and rear,
and they were kept many minutes in suspense. Then
they were marched on again towards *Campenhout*, surrounded by a company which, they were given to understand, was the "execution company." Crowds of
German troops, bivouacked by the roadside, shouted
at them and spat on them as they passed. They
reached *Campenhout* at dusk, and were locked up for
the night in the church with the inhabitants of the village. At 4.30 a.m. they were warned to confess, as
their execution was imminent. At 5.0 a.m. they were
released from the church, and told they were free. But
at *Bueken* they were arrested again with a large number of country people, and were marched back towards

---

*R1, 7, 26.
†R1, 8.
‡R26.

Campenhout. One of these countrywomen bore a baby
on the road.* From the outskirts of *Campenhout* they
were suddenly ordered to make their own way as best
they could to the Belgian lines. They arrived at
Malines about 11.30 in the morning (of August 27th),
about 200 strong. Within four hours of their arrival
the German bombardment† of *Malines* began, and they
had to march on again to *Antwerp*.

A second batch‡ was driven out along the *Brussels
Road* on August 26th between 1.0 and 2.0 o'clock in
the afternoon. As they marched through Louvain by
the *Rue de Bruxelles*, the guard fired into the windows of the houses and shot down one of the prisoners,
who was panic-stricken and tried to escape.§ At
Herent they were yoked to heavy carts and made to
drag them along by-roads for three hours,§ and another civilian was shot on the way.§ At 10.0 p.m.
they were made to lie down in an open field with their
feet tied together, and lay thus in pouring rain till 6.0
o'clock next morning. Then they were marched
through *Bueken, Thildonck, Wespelaer*—still in pouring rain—with their hands bound by a single long
cord. They reached *Campenhout* at noon, and were
set to digging trenches. At 7.0 p.m. they were allowed
to sit down and rest, but only just behind the batteries

---

* R7.
† R8.
‡ xxi p. 117; e18, 21; R22; "Germans" pp. 59-61.
§ e21.

bombarding the Antwerp forts,* which might have opened retaliation fire on them at any moment. That night they passed in Campenhout church, and at 9.0 o'clock next morning (August 28th) they were marched back again to Louvain, about 1,000 in all—women and children as well as men. "The houses along the road were burning. The principal streets of Louvain itself were burnt out."* That night at Louvain they were crowded into the *Cavalry Riding School* in the *Rue du Manège*. Six or seven thousand people were imprisoned there in all.† The press was terrible, and the heat from the burning buildings round was so great that the glass of the roof cracked during the night.† Two women went out of their minds and two babies died.‡ Next morning a German officer read them a proclamation to the effect that their liberty was given them because Germany had already won the war,§ and they were marched out again through the streets. They passed corpses left unburied since the night of August 25th.§ "The German soldiers giggled at the sight."‖ Once more they were driven round the countryside. At *Herent* the women and children, and the men over forty, were set free. At *Campenhout* the curé was added to the company, after being dragged round his

---

* e21.
† e18.
‡ R22; cp. e18, 21; "Germans" p. 60.
§ R22; e18.
‖ xxi p. 117.

parish at the tail of a cart.* At *Boortmeerbeek* the men between twenty and forty were also released at last, and told to go forward to the Belgian lines, under threat of being shot if they turned back. They arrived in front of *Fort Waelhem* in the dark, at 11.0 p.m. on the 29th, and were fired on by the Belgian outposts; but they managed to make themselves known and came through to safety.

The third batch "conveyed elsewhere" from Louvain on August 26th consisted of the Garde Civique.† All members of this body were summoned by proclamation to present themselves at the *Hôtel-de-Ville* at 2.0 p.m.‡ The 95 men who reported themselves were informed that they were prisoners, taken to the *Station*, and entrained in two goods-vans. There were 250 other deportees on the train, including the Gardes Civiques of *Beyghem* and *Grimberghen*, and about a hundred women and children. They did not reach the internment camp at *Münster* till the night of the 28th, and on the journey they were almost starved. At *Cologne Station* a German Red Cross worker refused one of the women, who asked her in German for a little milk to feed her sick baby fourteen months old.§ In the camp at *Münster* all the men were crowded pro-

---

* cp. p. 76 above.

† R23.

‡ Chambry p. 33; Grondijs p. 47.

§ A German soldier was so much shocked at this that he fetched the milk himself.

miscuously into a single wooden shed. The floor was
strewn with straw (already old), which was never
changed. The blankets (also old, and too thin to keep
out the cold) were never disinfected or washed. There
was no lighting or heating. The food was insufficient
and disgusting. The sanitary arrangements were in-
decent. And the deportees had to live under these
conditions for months, in the clothes they stood in,
though many had come in slippers and shirt-sleeves—
the proclamation having taken them completely by
surprise. In neighbouring huts there were the 400
Russian students from *Liége*, 600 or 700 people from
Visé, the Gardes Civiques of *Hasselt* and *Tongres*,
people from *Haccourt* and from several communes in
the *Province of Limburg*—about 1,700 prisoners in
all. On October 4th an article in the *Berliner Tage-
blatt*, signed by a German general, admitted that
"only two of the prisoners at *Münster* were under sus-
picion of having fired"; but none of the prisoners from
Louvain were released till October 30th, and then only
cripples and men over seventy years of age. The rest
were retained, including a man with a wooden leg. . . .

The fourth batch of prisoners on August 26th started
about 3.0 o'clock in the afternoon, also by way of the
Boulevard de Diest and the *Malines Road*.* This
group seems to have been treated even more brutally
than the rest. One man was so violently mishandled

---

* e3=R15; R17.

that he fainted, and was carried in a waggon the first part of the way. He came to himself in time to see his own house burning and his wife waving him farewell. He was then thrown out of the waggon and made to go on foot. His bonds cut so deeply into his flesh that his arms lost all sensation for three days. The party was marched aimlessly about between *Herent, Louvain, Bueken*, and *Herent* again till 11.0 at night, when they had to camp in the open in the rain. They were refused water to drink. At 3.0 a.m. on August 27th they were driven on again, and marched till 3.0 p.m., when they arrived at *Rotselaer*. At *Rotselaer* they were shut up in the church—a company of 3,000 men and women, including all the inhabitants of the village. This respite only lasted an hour, and at 4.0 o'clock they started once more along the Louvain Road. They were destined for a still worse torment, which will shortly be described.

These preliminary expulsions on the 26th were followed up by more comprehensive measures on the morning of the 27th. Between 8.0 and 9.0 a.m. German soldiers went round the streets proclaiming from door to door: "Louvain is to be bombarded at noon; everyone is to leave the town immediately."* The people had no time to set their affairs in order or to prepare for the journey. They started out just as

---

* "Germans" pp. 52-4, 71; Chambry pp. 40-1, 73; "Horrors" pp. 40-1; Grondijs p. 52; "Eye-witness" p. 5; e2; R11; D31.

they were, fearing that the bombardment would overtake them before they could escape from the town.
The exodus was complete. About 40,000 people altogether were in flight,* and the majority of them
streamed towards the *Station Square*, where they had
been ordered to assemble, and then out by the *Boulevard de Tirlemont*, along the *Tirlemont Road*.

The Dominicans from the Monastery in the *Rue
Juste-Lipse* were expelled with the rest. "At the moment when they were leaving the Monastery an old
man was brought in seriously wounded in the stomach;
it was evident that he had but a few hours to live. A
German officer proposed to 'finish him off,' but was
deterred by the Prior. One of the monks attempted to
pick up a paralysed person who had fallen in the street;
the soldiers prevented him, striking him with the butt-
ends of their muskets. The weeping, terrified population was hurrying towards the *Railway Station*. . . ."†
At the *Station* the Dominicans were stopped and sent
to Germany by train; the rest of the crowd was driven
on. There were from 8,000 to 10,000 people in this
first column.‡ "Nothing but heads was to be seen—
a sea of heads. . . . The wind was blowing violently,
and a remorseless rain scourged us. . . . The crowd
was pressing upon us, suffocating us, and sometimes

---

* "Germans" p. 54.
† xxi p. 116.
‡ R11.

literally lifting us along like a wave, our feet not touching the ground. We progressed with difficulty, and had to stop every ten metres. Sometimes a German asked us if we had any arms. . . ."* When they arrived at *Tirlemont* they were kept outside the town till nightfall.† The inhabitants did their best for them, but *Tirlemont*, too, had been ravaged by the invasion. The number of the refugees was overwhelming, and there was a dearth of supplies. "My mother and I," states a Professor of Louvain University,‡ "had to walk about 20 miles on the 27th and the following day before we could find a peasant cart. We had to carry the few belongings we were able to take away, and to walk in the heavy rain. We could find nothing to eat, but other people were yet more unfortunate than we. I saw ladies walking in the same plight, without hats and almost in their night-dresses. Sick persons, too, dragged themselves along or were carried in wheel-barrows. Thousands of people were obliged to sleep in *Tirlemont* on the church pavements. We found a little room to sleep in. . . ."

Ecclesiastics were singled out for special maltreatment. This professor, and twelve other priests or monks with him, was stopped by German troops encamped at *Lovenjoul*. They were informed that they

---

* Chambry pp. 53-4.
† R11.
‡ e2.

were going to be shot for "having incited the population."—"A soldier," states the professor, "called me
'Black Devil' and pushed me roughly into a dirty little
stable."—"I was thrust into a pig-stye," states one of
his fellow-victims,* "from which a pig had just been
removed before my eyes. . . . There I was compelled
to undress completely. German soldiers searched my
clothes and took all I had. Thereupon the other ecclesiastics were brought to the stye; two of them were
stripped like me; all were searched and robbed of all
they had. The soldiers kept everything of value—
watches, money and so on—and only returned us
trifles. Our breviaries were thrown into the manure.
Some of the ecclesiastics were robbed of large sums—
one had 6,000 francs on him, another more than 4,000.
All were brutally handled and received blows." They
were saved from death by the professor's mother, who
appealed to a German officer with more sense of justice
than his colleagues, and they were thankful to rejoin
the other refugees.

A second stream of refugees was pouring out of
Louvain by the *Tervueren Road*,† towards the south-
west. "On the road," states a professor,‡ "we had to
raise our arms each time we met soldiers. An officer

---

* R12.
† "Eye-witness" pp. 5-9; "Germans" p. 58; Grondijs pp. 61-71
(=R14); Chambry p. 73; R4, 13, 21 (=xxi pp. 117-9; "Eye-witness"
pp. 8-9).
‡ R13.

in a motor-car levelled his revolver at us. He threatened fiercely a young man walking by himself who only raised one arm—he was carrying a portmanteau in the other hand, which he had to put down in a hurry. At *Tervueren* we were searched several times over, and then took the electric tram for Brussels. . . ."

But here the ecclesiastics were singled out once more. One was searched so roughly that his cassock was torn from top to bottom.* Another was charged with carrying "cartridges," which turned out to be a packet of chocolates.† One soldier tried to slip a cartridge into a Jesuit's pocket, but the trick was fortunately seen by another monk standing by.‡ Insults were hurled at them—"Swine"; "Beastly Papists"; "You incite the people to fire on us"; "You will be castrated, you swine!" Then they were driven into a field, and surrounded by a guard with loaded rifles. About 140 ecclesiastics were collected altogether,§ including Mgr. Ladeuze, the Rector of Louvain University; Canon Cauchie, the Professor of History; Mgr. Becker, the Principal of the American Seminary; and Mgr. Willemsen, formerly President of the American College. After they had waited an hour, 26 of them were taken and lined up against a fence. Expecting to be shot, they gave one another absolution, but after waiting

* R22.
† "Eye-witness" p. 5.
‡ R21.
§ "Eye-witness" p. 6.

seven or eight minutes they were marched out of the field and lined up once more with their backs to a wood. As they marched, a soldier muttered that "one of them was going to be shot." The two Americans showed their passports to an officer, but were violently rebuffed. Then Father Dupierreux, a Jesuit student 23 years old, was led before them under guard, and one of their number was called forward to translate aloud into German a paper that had been found on Father Dupierreux's person. The paper (it was a manuscript memorandum of half-a-dozen lines) compared the conduct of the Germans at Louvain to the conduct of Genseric and of the Saracens, and the burning of the Library to the burning of the Library at Alexandria. The officer cut the recitation short. Father Dupierreux received absolution, and was then ordered to advance towards the wood. Four soldiers were lined up in front of him, and the 26 prisoners were ordered to face about, in order to witness the execution. Among their number was Father Robert Dupierreux, the twin brother of the condemned.* "Father Dupierreux," states Father Schill,† the Jesuit who had been forced to translate the document, "had listened to the reading with complete calm. . . . He kept his eyes fixed on the crucifix. . .. . The command rang out: 'Aim! Fire!' We only heard one report. The Father fell

---

* R21; "Eye-witness" p. 7.
† R21.

on his back; a last shudder ran through his limbs. Then the spectators were ordered to turn about again, while the officer bent over the body and discharged his pistol into the ear. The bullet came out through the eye."

The others were then placed in carts, and harangued:* "When we pass through a village, if a single shot is fired from any house, the whole village will be burnt. You will be shot and the inhabitants likewise." They were paraded in these carts through the streets of *Brussels* and liberated, at 7.0 o'clock in the evening, at eight kilometres' distance beyond the city.

Meanwhile, the proclamation of the morning had had its effect. Louvain was cleared of its inhabitants, but the bombardment did not follow. Between 11.0 and 12.0 o'clock a few cannon shots were heard in the distance, but that was all.† "At *Rotselaer*," states an inhabitant of Louvain who was in the party conveyed there on the 27th,‡ "I understood from the prisoners in the church that all the people of *Rotselaer* were made to leave their houses on the pretext that they were in danger of bombardment, and the Germans stated that they were being placed in the church for security. While all these people were in the church the Germans robbed the houses and then burned the

---

* R21.
† "Germans" p. 72; "Horrors" p. 42; cp. Chambry p. 56.
‡ e3.

village." At Louvain the German strategy was the same. The bombardment was only a pretext for the wholesale expulsion of the inhabitants, which was followed by systematic pillage and incendiarism as soon as the ground was clear. The conflagration of two nights before, which had never burnt itself out, was extended deliberately and revived where it was dying out; the plundering, which had been desultory since the Germans first occupied the town, was now conducted under the supervision of officers from house to house.*

On the morning of August 27th, even before the exodus began, a Dutch witness† waiting at the *Hôtel-de-Ville* saw "soldiers streaming in from all sides, laden with huge packages of stolen property—clothes, boxes of cigars, bottles of wine, etc. Many of these men were drunk."—"I saw the German soldiers taking the wine away from my house and from neighbours' houses," states a Belgian witness.‡ "They got into the cellar with a ladder, and brought out the wine and placed it on their waggons."—"The streets were full of empty wine bottles," states another.§ "My factory has been completely plundered," states a cigar-manufacturer.‖ "Seven million cigars have disap-

---

* R24.
† "Grondijs" p. 51.
‡ e4.
§ e8.
‖ R10.

143

peared." The factory itself was set on fire on the
26th, and was only saved by the Germans for fear the
flames might spread to the prison. They saved it by
an extinguishing apparatus which was as instantaneous
in its effect as the apparatus they used for setting houses
alight. "The soldiers, led by a non-commissioned
officer, went from house to house and broke in the shop
fronts and house doors with their rifle butts. A cart
or waggon waited for them in the street to carry away
the loot."* Carts were also employed in the suburb
of *Blauwput*, on the other side of the railway. "I saw
German soldiers break into the houses," states a witness from *Blauwput*.† "One party consisting of six
soldiers had a little cart with them. I saw these break
into a store where there were many bottles of champagne and a stock of cigars, etc. They drank a good
deal of wine, smoked cigars, and carried off a supply
in the cart. I saw many Germans engaged in looting."
This employment of carts became an anxiety to the
Higher Command. A type-written order, addressed
to the Officers of the 53rd Landwehr Infantry, lays
down that "For the future it is forbidden to use army
carts for the transport of things which have nothing
whatever to do with the service of the Army. At some
period these carts, which travel empty with our Army,
will be required for the transport of war material.

---

* R24.
† e26.

They are now actually loaded with all sorts of things, none of which have anything to do with military supplies or equipment."*

This systematic pillage went on day after day. "The *Station Square*," states a refugee from Louvain† who traversed the city again on August 29th, "was transformed into a vast goods-depôt, where bottles of wine were the most prominent feature. Officers and men were eating and drinking in the middle of the ruins, without appearing to be in the least incommoded by the appalling stench of the corpses which still lay in the *Boulevard*. Along the *Boulevard de Diest* I saw Landsturm soldiers taking from the houses anything that suited their fancy, and then setting the house alight, and this under their officers' eyes." On September 2nd there was a fresh outbreak of plunder and arson in the *Rue Léopold* and the *Rue Marie-Thérèse.*‡ As late as September 5th—ten days after the original catastrophe—the Germans were pillaging houses in the *Rue de la Station* and loading the loot on carts.§ Householders who returned when all was over found the destruction complete. "I found my parents' house sacked," states one.‖ "A great deal of the furniture was smashed, the contents of cupboards

---

* Chambry p. 86; v. p. 29.
† R11.
‡ "Germans" pp. 73, 89.
§ R10.
‖ R13.

and drawers were scattered about the rooms. . . .
In my sister's house the looking-glasses on the ground
floor were broken. On the bedding of the glass the
imprint of the rifle-butts was clearly visible."—"Inside our house," states another,* "everything is upside
down. . . . The floors are strewn with flowers and
with silver plate not belonging to our house, the writ-
ing room is filled with buckets and basins, in which
they had cooled the bottles of champagne. . . .
There was straw everywhere—in short, the place was
like a barn. To crown everything, my father was not
allowed to sleep in his own house. . . . When the
Germans at last quitted our residence, it was necessary
to cleanse and disinfect everything. The lowest stable
was cleaner than our bedrooms, where scraps from the
gourmandising and pieces of meat lay rotting in every
corner amid half-smoked cigars, candle ends, broken
plates, and hay brought from I don't know where."

But these two houses were, at any rate, not burnt
down, and more frequently, when they had finished
with a house, the Germans set it on fire. They had
begun on the night of August 25th; on August 26th
they were proceeding systematically,† and the work
continued on the 27th and the following days. All
varieties of incendiary apparatus were employed—a

* Chambry pp. 74-7.
† R19.

white powder,* an inflammable stick,† a projectile fired from a rifle.‡ They introduced these into the house to be burnt by staving in a panel of the front door § or breaking a window,‖ and the conflagration was immediate when once the apparatus was inside. This scientific incendiarism was the regular sequel to the organised pillage. The firing by German soldiers also went on. "On August 27th," states one German witness,¶ "I was fired at from a garden from behind the hedge, without being hit. It was in the afternoon; I could not see the person who had shot." The identification can be inferred from the experience of the Rector of Louvain University, Mgr. Ladeuze, on the night of August 25th, when he detected two German soldiers firing over the garden wall of the *Chemical Institute* into the *Rue de Namur*.** Another German witness, a military surgeon in the Neuss Landsturm,†† who arrived at Louvain in the afternoon of August 27th, testifies that "in the course of the afternoon I heard the noise of firing in the *Rue de la Station.* . . . I had the impression that we were being shot at from a house there, in spite of my conspicuous armlet with

* e16.
† R19.
‡ R24.
§ Chambry p. 52.
‖ R19.
¶ D19.
** "Germans" p. 107; Grondijs p. 58; cp. p. 105 above.
†† D21.

the Red Cross. We approached the house. A German soldier of another battalion leapt out from the first floor, and in so doing broke the upper part of his thigh. He told me that he had just been pursued and shot at by six civilians in the house." The surgeon, a young man of twenty-five, a new-comer to Louvain, and un-used to the notion of German soldiers firing on one another, repeats this story without seeing that it fails to explain the shots fired *from* the house and directed against himself, and he takes the presence of the "six civilians" on faith. Was the soldier who escaped punishment by this lie firing into the street from panic? This may have been so, for the German troops were in a state of nervous degeneration, but there is another possible explanation. Two days later, on August 29th, when Mr. Gibson, Secretary of the American Legation at Brussels, visited Louvain to enquire into the catas-trophe, his motor-car was fired at in the *Rue de la Station* from a house, and five or six armed men in civilian costume were dragged out of it by his escort and marched off for execution. But they were not executed, for they were German soldiers disguised to give Mr. Gibson an ocular demonstration that "the civilians had fired." The German Higher Command had already adopted this as their official thesis, and they were determined to impose it on the world.*

---

* R27 (Deposition of Mgr. Deploige, President of the *Institut Supérieur de Philosophie* and Director of the *Hôpital St.-Thomas*) ;

'After the exodus on the morning of the 27th, Louvain lay empty of inhabitants all day, while the burning and plundering went on. But at dusk a procession of civilians, driven by soldiers, streamed in from the north. They were the fourth batch of prisoners who had been marched out of Louvain on the previous day. They had spent the night in the open, and had been locked up that afternoon in *Rotselaer* church. But after only an hour's respite they had been driven forth again, and the whole population of *Rotselaer* with them, along the road leading back to the city.

"On the way," states one of the victims,* "we rested a moment. The curé of *Rotselaer*, a man 86 years of age, spoke to the officer in command: 'Herr Offizier, what you are doing now is a cowardly act. My people did no harm, and, if you want a victim, kill me. . . .' The German soldiers then seized the curé by the neck and took him away. Some Germans picked up mud from the ground and threw it in his face. . . ."

"We entered Louvain," states the curé himself,† "by the *Canal* and the *Rue du Canal*. No ruins. We reached the *Grand' Place*—what a spectacle! The *Church of Saint-Pierre!* Rest in front of the *Hôtel-de-Ville*. Fatigue compelled me to stretch myself on the pavement, while the houses blazed all the time.

R29 (Report by Abbé Van den Bergh, accredited by His Eminence Cardinal Piffl, Prince-Bishop of Vienna, to make enquiries on behalf of the Vienna Priester-Verein).

* e3. † R16.

"Other prisoners from Louvain and the neighbourhood kept arriving. Soon I saw fresh prisoners arrive from *Rotselaer*—women, children and old men, among others a blind old man of eighty years, and the wife of the doctor at *Rotselaer*, dragged from her sick-bed. (She died during the journey to Germany.) . . ."

"In the *Grand' Place*," states the former witness,* "the heat from the burning houses was so great that the prisoners huddled together to get away from it. . . ."

"After we had remained standing there about an hour," states a third,† "we had to proceed towards the *Station* along the *Rue de la Station*. In this same road we saw the German soldiers plundering the houses. They took pleasure in letting us see them doing it. In the city and at *Kessel-Loo* the conflagration redoubled in intensity."

"The houses were all burning in the *Rue de la Station*," states the first,‡ "and there were even flames in the street which we had to jump across. We were closely guarded by German soldiers, who threatened to kill us if we looked from side to side."

Yet these victims in their misery were accused of shooting by their tormentors. "On August 27th," states an officer concerned,§ "the Third Battalion of

---

* e3.
† R17.
‡ e3.
§ D34.

the Landwehr Infantry Regiment No. 53 had to take with it on its march from *Rotselaer* to Louvain a convoy of about 1,000 civilian prisoners. . . . Among the prisoners were a number of Belgian priests, one of whom,* especially caught my attention because at every halt he went from one to another of the prisoners and addressed words to them in an excited manner, so that I had to keep him under special observation. In Louvain we made over the prisoners at the *Station*. . . . On the following morning it was reported to me . . . that the above-mentioned priest had shot at one of the men of the guard, but had failed to hit him, and in consequence had himself been shot in the *Station Square*."

Such were the rumours that passed current in the German Army; but there is no reference in this officer's deposition to what really happened at the *Station* on the night of the 27th-28th. The prisoners arrived there about 7.0 p.m., and were immediately put on board a train. Their numbers had risen by now to between 2,000 and 3,000,† and the overcrowding was appalling. The curé of *Rotselaer* was placed in a truck which had carried troops and was furnished with benches; but even this truck was made to hold 50

* This was the Priest of *Herent*, the Abbé van Bladel, whose body was exhumed at *Louvain* on Jan. 14th, 1915, in the *Station Square* (R30).

† e5, 7, 17; R16.

people,* while the majority were forced into cattle
trucks—from 70 to 100 men, women, and children in
each,† which had never been cleaned, and were knee-
deep in dung.‡ They stood in these trucks all night,
while the train remained standing in the *Station*. On
August 28th, about 6.0 in the morning, they started
for *Cologne*, but the stoppages and shuntings were
interminable, and *Cologne* was not reached till the
afternoon of August 31st. During these four days—
from the evening of August 27th to the afternoon of
August 31st—the prisoners were given nothing to eat,§
and were not allowed to get out of the train to relieve
themselves when it stopped.‖ "We had nothing to
eat," states one of them,¶ "not even the child one
month old."—"My wife was suckling her child," states
another,** "but her milk came to an end. My wife was
crying nearly all the time. The baby was dreadfully
ill, and nearly died."—"We had been without food
for two days and nights, and had nothing to drink till
we got to *Cologne*, except that one of my fellow-
prisoners had a bottle of water, from which we just
wetted our lips."††—"I asked for some water for my

* R16; cp. e10.
† e3, 7, 17; "Germans" p. 68 (Narrative of a Bulgarian student).
‡ e3, 7, 10, 17; "Germans" p. 68.
§ e3, 5, 10; R17.
‖ e3, 7, 17.
¶ e3.
** e5.
†† e10.

child at *Aix-la-Chapelle*, and it was refused. It was the soldiers that I asked, and they spat at me when they refused the water. The soldiers also took all the money that I had upon me."*—"We had not been allowed to leave the train to obey the calls of nature, till at *Cologne* we went on our knees and begged the soldiers to allow us to get down."†

The brutality of the soldiers did not stop short of murder. "At *Henne*," where the train stopped at 3.30 a.m. on August 29th, "a man got out to satisfy nature. He belonged to the village of *Wygmael.* He was going towards the side of the line when three German soldiers approached him. One of them caught hold of him and threw him on the ground, and he was bayonetted by one or other of them in his left side. The man cried out; then the German soldier withdrew his bayonet and showed his comrades how far it had gone in. He then wiped the blood off his bayonet by drawing it through his hand. . . . After the soldier had wiped his bayonet, he and his comrades turned the man over on his face. . . . A few minutes after he had wiped his bayonet, he put his hand in his pocket and took out some bread, which he ate. . . ."‡

Between Louvain and the frontier two men in a passenger-carriage "tried to escape and broke the win-

---

* e5.
† e17.
‡ e10; confirmed by e11.

dows. The German sentinels bayonetted these two men and killed them."*

Two people on the train went mad,† and two committed suicide.‡ When the train started again after its halt at *Liége*, a man from *Thildonck* was run over, and it was supposed that he had thrown himself under the wheels to put himself out of his misery.§ When the train was emptied at *Cologne*, three of the prisoners were taken out dead.‖

The trucks were chalked with the inscription: "Civilians who shot at the soldiers at Louvain,"¶ and at every place in Germany where the train stopped the prisoners were persecuted by the crowd.** "At *Aix-la-Chapelle*," states the curé of *Rotselaer*, "an officer came up to spit on me."†† At *Aix*, too, those destined for the internment camp at *Münster* had to change trains and were marched through the streets. "As we went," states one of them,‡‡ "the German women and children spat at us."—"We arrived at *Aix-la-Chapelle*," states another witness.§§ "There the German people shouted at us. At *Dürren*, between *Aix-la-*

---

* e5.
† e3; cp. e7; R17.
‡ e3.
§ e10, 11.
‖ e16.
¶ e16.
** e10.
†† R16.
‡‡ e5.
§§ e3=R15.

Chapelle and *Cologne*, 4,000 German people crowded round. I turned round to the old woman with eight children, and said: 'Do these people think we are prisoners? Show them one of your little children, at the window.' This child was a month old, and naked. When the child was shown at the window a hush came over the crowd."

"When we reached *Cologne* a crowd came round the trucks, jeering at us, and as we marched out they prodded us with their umbrellas and pelted us and shouted: 'Shoot them dead! Shoot them dead!'— and drew their fingers across their throats."*

"At *Cologne*," states the curé of *Rotselaer*,† "we had to leave the train and parade—men, women and children—through the streets under the surveillance of the police."—"On the way," adds another,‡ "the children in the streets threw stones at us."

They were herded for the night into an exhibition-ground called the "Luna Park," and here their first food was served out to them—for every ten persons one loaf of mouldy bread.§ A certain number found shelter in a "joy-wheel"; the rest spent the night in the open, in the rain. The guards amused themselves by making individuals kneel down in turn and threat-

---

* e7; cp. e10.
† R16; cp. e10; R17; "Germans" p. 68.
‡ e17.
§ e17; R16.

ening them with execution.* Next morning they were marched back to the station, once more under the insults of the crowd, and started to retrace their journey, but not all of them were allowed to return. A batch of 300 men were kept at *Cologne* for a week, during which time 60 of their number were shot before the eyes of the rest, while the survivors were paraded through the town again and subjected more than once to a sham execution.† Others‡ were sent direct from *Aix-la-Chapelle* to the internment camp at *Münster,* where the Garde Civique of Louvain had been sent before. In this camp the men were separated completely from the women and children—one of them was the man§ whose baby had nearly died on the way, and for six weeks he was kept in ignorance of what was happening to the baby and to his wife. For the first six weeks they were given no water to wash in, and no soap during the whole period of their imprisonment. They were not allowed to smoke or read or sing. This particular prisoner was allowed by special grace to return to Louvain with his family on December 6th, but the others still remained.

Meanwhile, the main body of the prisoners was being transported back to Belgium. This return journey was almost as painful as the journey out; they

* R15.
† e16.
‡ e5.
§ e5.

were almost as badly crowded and starved;* but the
delays were less, and they reached *Brussels* on September 2nd. While they were halted at *Brussels*, Burgomaster Max managed to serve out to each of them a
ration of white bread.† They were carried on to
Schaerbeek, detrained, and marched in column to *Vilvorde*. "I was in the last file," states one of them.‡
"We were made to run quickly, and the soldiers struck
us on the back with their rifles and on the arms with
their bayonets."—"On the way to *Vilvorde* one man
sprang into the water, a canal—he was mad by then.
The German soldiers threw empty bottles at this man
in the water; they were bottles they got from the houses
as they passed, and were drinking from on the way."§
At *Vilvorde* they were informed that they were free.∥
They dragged themselves forward towards the Belgian
lines, but at *Sempst* another party of Germans took
them prisoner again.∥ "The Germans thrust their
bayonets quite close to our chests," states one of the
prisoners;¶ "then four of them prepared to shoot us,
but they did not shoot. One of the prisoners went
mad; I was made to hold him, and he hurt me very
much." Finally the officer commanding the picket let

---

* e3.
† e7, 10, 17; R16, 17.
‡ e17; cp. e3; R15, 16, 17.
§ e7; R16, 17.
∥ e3, 17; R15.
¶ e17.

them go once more. They asked if they might return to Louvain. "If you go back that way we will kill you," the officer said; "you have to go that way," and he pointed towards *Malines.** It was now midnight, and pouring with rain. The prisoners stumbled on again, and made their way, in scattered parties, to the Belgian outposts.†

This horrible railway journey to *Cologne* was the last stroke in the campaign of terrorisation carried out against Louvain after the night of August 25th by the deliberate policy of the German Army Command. A refugee who had returned to the city on August 28th, and had been kept prisoner during the night, was released with her fellow prisoners on the 29th. "We will not hurt you any more," said the officer in command; "stay in Louvain. All is finished."‡

On August 30th the staff of the *Hôpital St.-Thomas*, who had defied the proclamation of the 27th and remained continuously at their posts, took the task of reconstruction in hand.§ A committee of notables was formed, and overtures were made to Major von Manteuffel, the German Etappen-Kommandant in the town. On September 1st a proclamation, signed by the provisional municipal government, was posted up,

* e3; R15.
† R16.
‡ e13.
§ "Germans" p. 84 *seqq.;* R27.

THE DIARY OF GASTON KLEIN

With von Manteuffel's sanction, in the streets.* It communicated a promise from the German Military Authorities that pillage and arson should thenceforth cease, and it invited the inhabitants to come back to Louvain and take up again their normal life. The most pressing task was to clear the ruins, and to find and bury the dead. In Louvain alone, not including the suburban communes, 1,120 houses had been destroyed and 100 civilians had been killed during this week of terror.

"We arrived at Louvain," writes a German soldier in his diary on August 29th.† "The whole place was swarming with troops. Landsturmers of the Halle Battalion came along, dragging things with them— chiefly bottles of wine—and many of them were drunk. A tour round the town with ten bicyclists in search of billets revealed a picture of devastation as bad as any imaginable. Burning and falling houses bordered the streets; only a house here and there remained standing. Our tour led us over broken glass, burning wood-work and rubble. Tram and telephone wires trailed in the streets. Such barracks as were still standing were full up. Back to the *Station*, where nobody knew what to do next. Detached parties were to enter the streets, but actually the Battalion marched in close order into

* "Germans" p. 86; R27.
† Ann. 8 (Extract from the Diary of Gaston Klein); cp. Bryce p. 80, No. 32.

the town, to break into the first houses and loot—
of course, only to 'requisition'—for wine and ot
things. Like a wild pack they broke loose, each
their own; officers set a good example by going
ahead. A night in a barracks with many drunk v
the end of this day, which aroused in me a conten
I cannot describe."

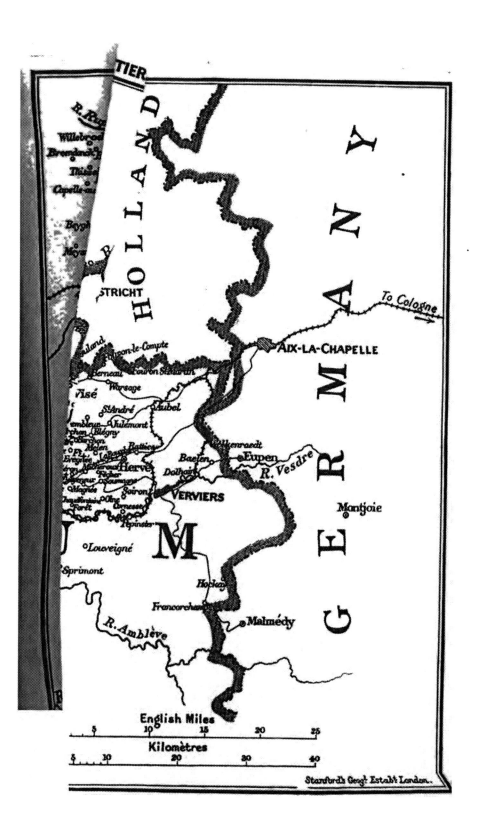

TIER

R. Roer

HOLLAND

Willebroe...

Broegbrock

Thiss...

Capelle-au...

Beyg...

Meuse

...STRICHT

To Cologne

...land

...gon-le-Compte

Berneau ...ouron Slatarin

Visé Wareage

St André Aubel

...mblewe Julémont

...chen Blégny

...Barchon ...gen Battice

Evegnée Fl...

...Micheroul Herve

...Baelen Eupen

...court Fol... Dolhain

Magnée Soiron R. Vesdre

...lis O'Hne Ornesse VERVIERS

Forêt Pepinster

Louveigné M

Montjoie

Sprimont

Hoc...

Francorcha...

R. Amblève Malmédy

AIX-LA-CHAPELLE

...enraedt

G E R M A N Y

English Miles
5   10   15   20   25

Kilomètres
5   10   20   30   40

Stanford's Geogl Estabt London.

Printed in the United States
109713LV00001B/173/A